Hearthstrings

Hearthstrings

How to Make Decorative Garlands
for All Seasons

CAROL CRUESS PFLUMM

Paintings by
BEVERLY DUNCAN

Foreword by Julee Rosso

VIKING
STUDIO
BOOKS

VIKING STUDIO BOOKS
Published by the Penguin Group
Penguin Books USA Inc., 375 Hudson Street,
New York, New York 10014, U.S.A.
Penguin Books Ltd, 27 Wrights Lane, London W8 5TZ, England
Penguin Books Australia Ltd, Ringwood, Victoria, Australia
Penguin Books Canada Ltd, 10 Alcorn Avenue,
Toronto, Ontario, Canada M4V 3B2
Penguin Books (N.Z.) Ltd, 182–190 Wairau Road,
Auckland 10, New Zealand

Penguin Books Ltd, Registered Offices:
Harmondsworth, Middlesex, England

First published in 1993 by Viking Penguin,
a division of Penguin Books USA Inc.

1 3 5 7 9 10 8 6 4 2

Grateful acknowledgment is made for permission to reprint "Wildings (Ebenecook,
Maine, 1969)" from *Herbs of a Rhyming Gardener* by Elisabeth W. Morss.
By permission of Branden Publishing, Boston.

ISBN: 0-670-84244-3

CIP data available

Printed in Singapore
Set in Goudy and Goudy Newstyle

Designed by Francesca Belanger

To my mother, Priscilla Pelland Cruess,
who encouraged me to begin;
Paul, Kristin, and Nina,
who sustained me;
Mary Milligan,
who made me one of her siblings;
and my Scottish sisters,
who made me
their own.

Contents

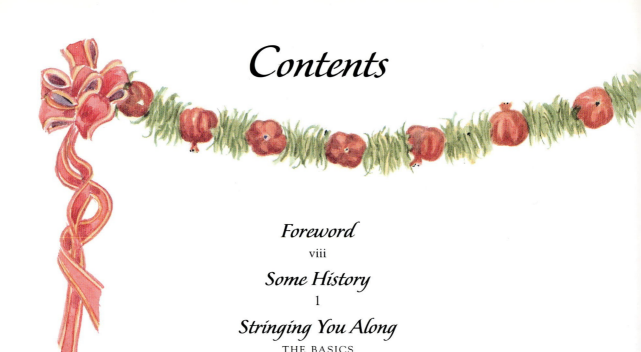

Strings for the Christmas Tree

Decorative Country Strings

Romantic Rose Strings

Woodland Strings

Scrapbook Strings

Sources

Foreword

I've long believed that fruits, vegetables, nuts, seeds, and herbs have a beauty all their own; I love using them for purposes that are decorative as well as culinary. Gathered from field and forest, garden and glen, the same bounty that satisfies the appetite can fill the house with a fanciful array of shapes and textures, the scent of seasons past, and a comforting presence that reminds us of the age-old tradition of "putting by." Whether heaped in a bowl or strung in garlands across the hearth, the fruits of the harvest create a kind of still life made tangible. They offer a connection with the earth and with the past, as much as canning tomatoes on a steamy August afternoon or gathering apples to dry in the crisp air of autumn.

In this book, Carol Pflumm combines her appreciation for bounty and beauty with her great sense of style, blending homespun traditions with a sophisticated eye for color and form. She invents garlands of every fruit and herb imaginable, laurels for every season and celebration—all put together with an eye for form and texture, and most having heady scents that speak of summer's charms long after the garden has withered away. Some of these Hearthstrings possess a rustic charm; others the sophistication and style to complement the most contemporary tastes. Like nature, they harmonize with the seasons, making the most use of materials found, grown, and carefully chosen from the garden for the perfect effect.

Hearthstrings offer the satisfaction of making something simple and natural with one's own hands—the kinds of objects that contribute to that indefinable sense of "home." With the author's easy-to-follow instructions, anyone can put together these strings of garden "treasures," often in less time than it would take to make a favorite recipe.

But this is more than just a "how-to" book: the author sprinkles the narrative with charming remembrances of family and friends and glimpses into the quality of life in small towns across the country. Recipes, crafts, and lore handed down from generation to generation, observations about the garden and countryside, and portraits of the author's country neighbors make *Hearthstrings* a book that reflects the warmth and sturdy simplicity of country living.

I see *Hearthstrings* as a blend of nostalgia and ingenuity—an ode to those who preserve the ways of the past with a flair of their own.

—Julee Rosso

Some History

*I*n colonial America, frugal housewives made canny use of every sort of food they could save for the hungry, soul-trying winters. There is no record of the first settlers stringing foodstuffs at the Plymouth settlement, but it was not long before food was put up by salting, preserving, and drying. In early, simple dwellings, drying was done by stringing chunks and slices of fruits and vegetables to hang near the warmth of the open hearth. In her book *Colonial Kitchens: Their Furnishings and Their Gardens*, Frances Phipps studied inventories of early kitchens, which show how little the average householder owned and how precious were even the simplest things. She quotes Peter Kalm's 1770 *Travels in America*:

> Pumpkins were cut in slivers, drawn up on a thread and dried [to] keep all year long and are boiled or stewed.

Other accounts tell of drying apples, cherries, peaches, berries, beans, pumpkins, and squash.

Dried beans and apples are good keepers, so from colonial times until the day of the modern freezer they were staples of winter eating. During the nineteenth century, the Pennsylvania Dutch dried their abundant apple crops, soaking them when they wanted to reconstitute the apples for baking or stewing. The Pennsylvanians called dried apple slices *schnitz*. In antique shops from Vermont to the Midwest, slatted wooden *schnitz* dryers, once used in every rural household, still turn up. The *schnitz* were placed on the dryer and left out in the sun, or sometimes put in a drying house similar to a smokehouse.

Schnitz are still made by the Pennsylvania Dutch and the Amish and sold in regional markets. Preserving foods by sun drying as well as in electric dehydrators has continued well into this century. During the second World War, many families, even city dwellers, kept Victory gardens and used basement cold storage rooms for storing squash, carrots, parsnips, and other root vegetables. Home-canned foods were kept in the pantry to ease the burden of wartime rationing. Although American women continue to be canny and practical, the stringing of any sort of foodstuffs for drying has long since faded into history, just as the open hearth has given way to the comforts of central heating and the Westinghouse range.

When, in 1821, the first Christmas tree in America was written about in a Lancaster, Pennsylvania, newspaper, a whole new category of purely decorative strings was born. A decade later, trees festooned with fruit and nut strings were frequently mentioned in newspaper accounts and personal letters.

My own journey to creating Hearthstrings began in 1967, after I moved to a nineteenth-century house in a very out-of-the-way village in Massachusetts (population: 1,000). With little money but boundless energy and excitement, my husband and I learned to do every kind of fix-up and restoration job. There were some lilacs and some quince on the property, but mostly there were big, open flat expanses that cried out for attention.

With some birthday pocket money from my kind mother-in-law, I went off to

a luncheon at Caprilands Herb Farm in rural Connecticut, one of the oldest and best-known herb farms in America. I carefully spent my money on a few plants. As she spoke to her guests, Adelma Simmons, Caprilands' resident writer and grower of herbs, captured my imagination. Her life at Caprilands seemed ideal: She was the very model of a gentlewoman gardener, cook, and scholar. I knew that was exactly what I wanted to be! Awaiting the birth of my third and youngest child, I gardened passionately all day and retired at night to read everything I could lay my hands on. It was a period of great happiness for me.

With weekend help in the garden and encouragement from my husband, I soon began selling herb plants—not readily available to the general public in 1969. Later, more herbs and my own dried flower designs were sold in room settings at antique shows. Then a friend told me about another gardener-businesswoman, Barbara Rogers, who was harvesting and drying pomegranates in California. Improbably, sitting at a seaside cottage in Maine during a heat wave in July, I boldly ordered an inordinate amount of them for fall delivery. What a turning point for me! As soon as I placed the order, I was captivated by the color and charm of these new products, and knew I wanted to put on my thinking cap and design a product myself. Years before, I had seen apple strings drying when I had taken my children to Old Sturbridge Village, near my mother and father's home in central Massachusetts. A more vivid memory of golden paper chains made for my first Christmas tree in a little apartment years before made me put two and two together. With a strong sense of history and a bit of invention, I began stringing dozens and dozens of pomegranates with fresh bay to make holiday garlands. They caused a sensation!

Some years later, *Victoria* magazine photographed my garden looking its misty untamed best. It is a garden of natural abundance, with every space planted to leave no room for weeds. The photographs were taken on a rainy June morning, when the old roses were in bloom. The sensitive heading the editors used at the top of the page read: *In Carol's Garden There are Many Memories*. In *Hearthstrings*, I share my imaginings and my memories with you.

When my son, my oldest child, was a very small boy, our local newspaper photographed us making clove-studded apple pomanders together for one of their Christmas features. His dimpled smile and deep concentration in that faded clipping capture a moment. We were using our hands to make something simple and natural at Christmas.

My middle child, now a beautiful young woman with the delicate features and flowing tresses of an early Renaissance portrait, is our family artist. Her imagination and skill have been a wonder to us all. Her Christmas gifts are always original and homemade as well as beautifully wrapped in papers of her own design. In creativity, it is she who sets the standard for her elders.

When my youngest child was attending our village school, they had a Valentine Box in which everybody dropped a card. Every year my younger daughter and I got down our box of flower stickers—forget-me-nots and lily-of-the-valley—and paper doilies. Then we mixed up a batch of homemade flour-and-water paste and made our own valentines. These times brought us close together and gave us a respect for accomplishment and frugality that we now share as adults.

Now you know how my small herb garden grew over the course of 20 years into an adventure and inspired me to write a book on making decorative Hearthstrings. Once you start seeing natural objects in terms of how they would look in a string, and once you open your eyes to the stringing possibilities inherent in every growing season and walk in the park, you will think of many more. As you make these strings, you will find lasting satisfaction.

Stringing You Along

THE BASICS

*T*here are certain steps common to all the project "recipes" in this book. From your shopping list to suggestions for hanging finished garlands, this introductory chapter will tell you everything you need to know; read it before you begin.

First, assemble your materials in an inviting workspace so you will enjoy yourself as you work! You will want good light, a comfortable chair, and a roomy flat surface to spread out your materials.

When you are ready to begin a string, choose thin but sturdy natural cord of cotton, linen, jute, or hemp—generically called "twine" in all the recipes hereafter. Fishing line, available at sporting-goods stores, also works well because it supports weight yet allows flexibility so that a finished Hearthstring drapes easily. Fiber-covered freshwater fishing line is nice to work with. Some people like to work with clear nylon line. It is very inexpensive and easily bought at sporting-goods or even hardware stores, but beware: It can give nasty little cuts to leaves and your hands.

For the lightest-weight strings, like rose hips or raisins or most of the Christmas-tree strings, heavy sewing thread labeled "Coat and Button" works well. Needlework and stationery shops, hardware stores, kitchenware shops, and garden centers often have a good selection of thread or natural fiber twine.

Then, decide what length you would like your finished Hearthstring to be. Measure the twine you are using to the desired finished length plus a generous allowance to make loops at each end for hanging. A safe allowance is 6 to 8 inches longer than the desired length. For example, if you want a finished string of 24 inches, cut the twine you'll be working with to about 32 inches.

Tie a loop at one end of the string and secure it with a good sturdy knot. Then thread the other end of the string through the eye of a large-eyed needle. The basic method is to puncture the materials with your needle and gently push them onto the string.

Tapestry needles, available at needlework shops, are a good choice for most projects because they are blunt and save annoying little stabs as you work. For safety when working on these projects with small children, you can use a plastic yarn needle with a large eye. But since a plastic needle is soft, it cannot be used on all materials.

With some of the natural materials used in the projects, pine cones and soft pieces of driftwood, for example, you will need a sharp-ended needle. Long rug or upholstery needles, or darning needles, usually sold in the notions sections of department stores, are suitable for this purpose. With some of the harder, denser materials, like pine cones or rose hips, a tack hammer might be useful for tapping the needle through the difficult parts of the object.

Until you have gained some experience, a good length for most Hearthstrings is 36 inches. Longer lengths can become unmanageable and tangle while you work. As you gain experience and confidence, longer projects made to measure will become a welcome challenge. Yards of strings can drape a doorway, garland a holiday staircase, or be adapted for pew decorations at a country wedding.

Push pins are a good way to hang finished strings, or to join sections. The loops tied at each end should be large enough to go over the head of a push pin or small nail easily, but not any larger than that. Keep the loops unobtrusive unless the color or texture of the twine you choose adds to the overall design.

All Hearthstrings look their best when hung out of direct sunlight and away from moisture.

"A friend may well be reckoned the Masterpiece of Nature."

—*Ralph Waldo Emerson*

Decorations and Celebrations

DRIED CRAB APPLES

Strings of dried apples are seasonal pleasures. In September, the tall ladders and big wooden boxes go out under the apple trees at the orchard. The days are sunny, but the air is crisp with the feeling that frost may come any time. We light our fireplace for the first time and begin nestling in again. That's when it's time to start making dried apple strings, which will keep well into late spring. When you take down your strings in June, you will miss their wintertime fragrance, fruity and comforting like warmed cider on a cold night.

Some country villages still have stores where they age great wheels of cheddar and offer Gravensteins, Red Astrakans, and other old varieties of apples our grandmothers knew. If you are lucky, there will be tart little crab apples too. A generation ago, when jelly making was a regular part of the fall season and jelly cupboards were fully stocked, crab apple jelly was always a favorite. Now crab apples are harder to find. Any firm apple can be cut thin with your favorite paring knife in random uneven slices and dried for stringing. (If apples are soft they will not slice properly.) Hand cutting your apples gives them a ruffled edge as they dry that is pleasing. It is worth the extra effort. So forget the clever kitchen timesavers for this project and keep a sharp edge on your knife.

INSTRUCTIONS FOR DRYING

There are three basic ways to dry natural materials for stringing. With some fruits or vegetables, one method is preferable to another. Sometimes your climate, the tools you have at hand, or your patience will help you decide which way to jump into this adventure. These explicit instructions will guide you in choosing the best method for you.

1. Screens for Air Drying

Whole fruits such as pomegranates and artichokes can be air dried in a single layer in a bowl or basket in any warm, dry room in about two weeks with fine results and no further attention from you. Fruit slices are trickier and require screens and warmth.

Drying fruit on screens will make you feel like you are recapturing something special from the past. Apple slices, for example, should be cut thin, but not paper thin, and spread out in a single layer, whether on a screen or in a dehydrator or oven. After they are cut, your screen can be placed in the warm sun on those golden days that come along in autumn, or in an attic room. Humidity in the air is an enemy to good drying results. In California, raisins, apricots, and apples are sun-dried on cloudless days and rain is seldom a problem. But for most readers, outdoor drying is as chancy as the weather and can take two weeks or even longer.

2. Dehydrator

A commercial electric food dehydrator is a wonderful tool to use because it gives you control of heat as well as air circulation. Round carousel-shaped models and larger-capacity square, multi-shelved dehydrators are available in housewares sections of department stores. When the machine is set at the

highest setting—135° F on my machine—apple slices will dry in 8 to 12 hours. Orange slices retain best color if dried at lower heat and require even more time. In either case, I set the timer for five or six hours, then check and reset. Fruit slices should be tough and leathery to the touch. If they are too dry, they will turn brittle and break, but if they are too moist and soft, you will be disappointed by spoilage.

3. Oven Drying

An oven set at less than 200° F does the trick with fruit slices, though slowly, and requires a lot of attention from you. Slices must be turned and checked often. The oven door should be kept slightly ajar to provide air, and that is very energy inefficient. For apples, I have found the timing difficult for that perfect leathery result—usually about 8-to-10 hours. Orange slices are quicker, sometimes ready in two hours, though they too can require as long as eight hours, so check often. Keep the heat low and don't try to hurry things along with higher heat. It will spoil the delicate color and cause browning.

Crab apples dry to mellow shades—the ivory and deep old red of hand-dyed quilts and coverlets. These colors are so rich that crab apples are worth the hunt. But if they just don't turn up, look for the smallest sizes of red or green apples in your neighborhood. If you can, go to an orchard. The little ones will be much less expensive than the choice big ones headed for city markets. Often, farmers will sell baskets of small apples reasonably. That's good news because apples under 2 inches in diameter are best for stringing.

30 crab apples

Sharp paring knife

Drying screens, electric food dehydrator,
    or slow oven

Tapestry needle with a large eye

32 inches strong thin twine

To assemble

Cut the apples horizontally into about 150 slices. Do not core the apples. Dry according to one of the methods described on pages 10–11.

The apples should be tough and leathery to the touch. If they are too dry, they will turn brittle and break, but if they are too moist and soft, you will be disappointed by spoilage.

Thread the needle with the twine and tie a loop at the other end. Gently push the needle through a dried apple slice and slide it to the end of the string. Repeat until all apple slices are strung. Ease—not quite push—the slices together as you work, and try to put the needle through the small holes that form around the core as seeds drop out in the drying process. It will save time and your fingers! To end, remove the needle, tie another loop, and knot securely.

Remembering

So often, people who love history are the very ones who find pleasure in cooking, tending a garden, and enriching their homes with antiques. My friend Pat Guthman writes a food column for a weekly newspaper and is equally at home entertaining 30 antiques dealers in town for a show or having an old friend over for backgammon and potluck. Pat's sense of adventure in her cooking led her to a serious study of open-hearth cookery. Central to her research was a study of the early iron tools used for cooking on an open hearth. Now, some years later, she and her daughter, Pam, have a gallery full of period furnishings for home and hearth.

Pat's career as an antiques dealer in tiny Southport, Connecticut, famous for its picturesque harbor and historic homes, involves her in many community events. One year, in the early winter, she set up a kitchen with an open hearth at the historical society benefit. From her shop, full of early iron cooking tools, she selected footed iron spiders, a trammel, and a fireplace crane, then hung porridge pots and a kettle from them to demonstrate what a colonial kitchen might have looked like.

YANKEE RECIPES FROM OLD VERMONT KITCHENS

Dried Apple Pie

Soak dried apples in water overnight, and stew till soft. Mash fine, add the grated peel of a lemon, and sweeten to taste with maple sugar. Bake with one bottom crust and strips of pastry on top.

The Green Mountain Cook Book
Brattleboro, Vermont
1941

Pat loves herbs, so she gave me a call for help. Together we hung historically accurate varieties to dry in her teaching kitchen. In keeping with her theme, she strung pumpkin chunks and bits of squash close by the fireside. Just over the hearth she hung string upon string of dried apples in her own version of the first early Hearthstrings. When you work together on a pet project with Pat, there's sure to be a little learning, a lot of laughing, and plenty of good things to eat!

Do you grow your own basil and parsley in summertime? Do you always feel let down by the color and flavor loss when you try to dry basil, parsley, or tarragon in the oven at home? Apple slices are not the only thing that dries to perfection in an electric dehydrator. Your dried herbs will never be the same! They will be greener and more flavorful than you ever dreamed dried herbs could be.

GREEN APPLES AND EUCALYPTUS

*T*hough they say that there is nothing new under the sun, we know that creativity comes from seeing old things in new ways. Sometimes new things come along and make creative thinking a little easier for us.

When the first seed catalogues arrive in our mailboxes each winter, there's a sense of discovery. New hybrids are developed each year, and old, nearly forgotten varieties are rediscovered. New worlds of opportunity open up! Each spring, the garden centers come alive with new shades of color and subtle fragrances for us to enjoy. Sometimes we walk through the garden trying to envision the wonderful changes that will ensue when we plant perennial sweet peas or pale green zinnias for the first time.

More cut flowers and fresh greens are available at flower shops now too. Not long ago, the only eucalyptus sold at the florist was the sort that grows in upright whorls around its stems (*Eucalyptus gunnii*). Unless it grows where you live, you sel-

dom saw soft green Silver Dollar Eucalyptus (*Eucalyptus cinerea*) or Flat Eucalyptus (*Eucalyptus tetragona*), a little grayer and broader leafed.

Silver Dollar
Eucalyptus

Flat
Eucalyptus

Common
Eucalyptus

Flat Eucalyptus is loved by flower arrangers for its attractive seed pods. In fact, it is sometimes called Seeded Eucalyptus and it is the *best* choice for stringing. You will find that the leaves are fuller and that each stem is heavy with leaves. Silver Dollar Eucalyptus is a suitable second choice. Because it has few leaves to the stem, *Eucalyptus gunnii*, the familiar variety so beautiful in dried arrangements, is unsuitable for making decorative Hearthstrings.

When you finish the string, hang it up and enjoy its beauty. As the eucalyptus ages, the leaves will dry and some will curl. The curling adds variation and texture. The color lasts and lasts.

If you enjoy the color and fragrance of these eucalyptus varieties while you are working on this string, you can use either of them in place of bay leaves to make any of the Hearthstrings that require greens. Although it has become quite popular and is widely sold in flower shops, eucalyptus may be harder to find and more costly than bay leaves. It is also a lighter green than bay leaves. But both eucalyptus and bay are lush when they are fresh and both dry nicely as they hang in your home.

"I would feel more optimistic about a bright future for man
if he spent less time proving he can outwit nature
and more time tasting her sweetness."

—*E.B. White*

to make one 36-inch Hearthstring

20 green apples
Sharp paring knife
Large bunch Flat or Silver Dollar Eucalyptus
Tapestry needle with a large eye
44 inches strong thin twine
Drying screens, electric food dehydrator, or slow oven
12 strands natural raffia, each one yard long

TO ASSEMBLE

Cut apples horizontally into 5 slices each. Dry according to instructions on pages 10–11. Check to be sure apple slices are flexible yet fully dry. Strip all eucalyptus leaves from their stems.

Thread the needle with the twine and tie a loop at the other end.

Push the needle through the center of a eucalyptus leaf and slide it to the end of the string. Follow with another leaf until you have about 4 inches of leaves. Then push the needle through the center of an apple slice and slide it next to the leaves. Follow with more apple slices until you have established a pattern of 4 inches of leaves followed by 4 inches of apples. Follow that pattern to the end. Always begin and end with leaves for a fuller look.

To end, remove the needle, tie another loop, then knot securely.

Holding 5 strands of raffia together, form a loopy bow by wrapping them back and forth between your thumb and forefinger in a figure 8. Tie in the middle with another raffia strand and attach to one end of the finished string. Repeat and attach to the other end of the string.

LITTLE GREEN APPLES

Let yourself be tempted! When they are just perfect at the market, bring home a bag of glossy green Granny Smith or Rhode Island Greening apples. Use the drying and stringing process on pages 10 –11 to make a green Hearthstring. You will be surprised when you finish what a contemporary look you have created just by making a different color choice.

SOME RED APPLES AND SOME GREEN

When you alternate short sections of dried red apple slices with dried green apple slices on a string, pretty things happen. Tiny under-size Red Delicious apples are often available and dry very nicely. Another fine variety that dries to a good color is Gala. After drying your apples, establish a pattern of red apples, then green, and repeat that pattern until you have completed the Hearthstring.

Remembering

Nancy and John Calhoun live on a llama farm in a Connecticut town where cars still cross the river on a covered bridge. In winter, Nancy's kitchen is sunny and inviting, the kind of place where the local school board meets and the children gather after school every day. Along one wall there's an antique pine Welsh dresser holding baskets she likes to fill with English primroses and cowslips blooming in soft pastel shades. Spilling out of other baskets and swagged along the shelves are strings of bright green apples. The colorful primula and dried green apples fill the room with springtime promise on the chilliest days.

GOLDEN ARTICHOKES AND BAY

*T*he two different plants that are given the common name artichoke are globe artichoke (*Cynara scolymus*), from the thistle family, and the Jerusalem artichoke (*Helianthus tuberosus*), a member of the sunflower clan. While it is actually not an artichoke at all, the Jerusalem artichoke produces a cheery sunflower blossom and its tubers, sometimes called sunchokes, are delicious to eat. It is a valuable cottage plant. Once planted, it produces food and flowers for years and years.

For making Hearthstrings, it is the true globe artichoke we want to use. The unripened flower head is the delicious part we eat and the one we string. Its form is one of classic beauty. The artichoke looks like its thistle-family cousin, the acanthus, which decorates Corinthian columns. The acanthus of ancient Greece is commonly called the silver thistle (*Acanthus spinosus*). Both the artichoke and the acanthus are majestic, large-leaved plants. The doyenne of English florists, Constance Spry, wrote that she could never decide whether to harvest artichokes for her table or for her famous London flower shop.

Globe artichokes are gilded to emphasize their natural elegance for this Hearthstring. You can save the drying step by purchasing wonderful miniature artichokes grown and dried in California (see Sources, page 95) and sold widely in herb and craft-supply shops.

The dried artichokes can be gilded using gold metallic spray paints from the hardware store or special florists' sprays. It's harder to brush liquid color into the nooks and crannies, but it can be done if you choose.

Another stylish look can be achieved by painting on the blue-green verdigris color that looks like aged copper, brass, or bronze. Trendy decorators call this painted finish *verde*. A verdigris paint kit can be bought from stores and mail-order catalogues or you can develop your own effect with three separate colors. To

do that, you brush or spray a base coat of metallic gold on the artichoke and let it dry. Then sponge on random spots of pale celadon green. Finally, after you have allowed time for previous coats to dry, pick up your sponge again to apply another random, uneven coat of metallic copper paint. The metallic copper paint can also be used alone for spectacular results.

YOU NEED
to make one 36-inch Hearthstring

12 fresh or dried small artichokes
Dust mask and protective gloves
Shallow box
Gold metallic spray paint
½ pound (about 300) fresh or dried bay leaves
Long rug needle with a sharp point
44 inches strong thin twine
1 yard elegant gold ribbon

TO ASSEMBLE

If using fresh artichokes, spread them out in a single layer to air dry naturally in a warm room. This will take a week or two.

Put on a dust mask to cover your nose and mouth and put gloves on your hands. Arrange the artichokes in a single layer in the bottom of a shallow box. Bring box outdoors and spray artichokes with gold paint. Allow to dry. Turn the artichokes and spray the other side. Allow to dry.

If using fresh bay leaves, strip the leaves from the branches and discard stems.

Thread the needle with the twine and tie a loop at the other end. Push the needle through the center of a bay leaf and slide it to the end of the string. Follow with more leaves until you have about 2 inches of leaves. Then push the needle through the center of the artichoke at its widest point and slide it down next to the leaves. Establish a pattern of 2 inches of leaves followed by an artichoke and continue to the end. Remove needle, tie another loop, and knot securely.

Cut the ribbon into 2 pieces, each 18 inches long. Tie to the string at each end after the last section of leaves, and form bow as though you were tying a shoelace, leaving the loops free.

Remembering

My grandmother Alexina Pelland was a country woman who raised 10 children with her husband, a farmer and a weaver. She had very little materially yet never seemed hungry for more. She might have come from the pages of Larkrise to Candleford or have been kin to Willa Cather's beloved Nebraska heroine Antonia. Yet she lived far from either place.

Alexina had a flock of grandchildren. All of us felt special in the company of this spiritual and humble woman, who nourished a sense of self-worth in each child. I remember that Alexina, whom I called Memere, gave me a little wooden chest, made by my grandfather, filled with a doll's wardrobe that she had fashioned from scraps of an aunt's old curtains.

Of all the grandchildren, however, it is Patricia who is most like her grandmother.

She shares Alexina's spirituality and love of the garden. She can also make something out of nothing with the same intuitive artistry. Patricia remembers trying to wake up at 5 o'clock on summer mornings, before her brother Larry, so she could help in our grandmother's garden. It was an immaculately weeded plot, a true cottage garden, full of tiny potatoes and crisp carrots growing alongside cosmos of every kind.

If you were the first to be on

> ## MEMERE'S TURKEY STUFFING
> *A True French Canadian Farmhouse Recipe*
>
> Peel, boil, then mash 5 pounds of potatoes.
>
> Mix well 1 pound lean ground beef with ½ pound lean ground pork. Chop a large onion and add to the meat mixture with 2 tablespoons water and brown slowly over the lowest heat until the liquid disappears, about 2 hours.
>
> Whip the potatoes until smooth. Add 2 tablespoons chopped fresh or dried sweet marjoram, salt and pepper to taste, 4 tablespoons butter, and then fold in the meat mixture.

hand, the reward was a lunch of fresh vegetables with Grandmother all to yourself. As Alexina grew older, her family would ask why she still did such hard work. "Never mind," Alexina would say with a rabbit-like wrinkle of her nose. She used to scoff at such nonsense. If they didn't understand that little, freshly dug vegetables were reward enough, there was no use explaining it. But Patricia understood. They would go off together to pick blackberries in the patch of woods that separated their houses.

Today, Patricia makes Hearthstrings and grows cosmos. I, the granddaughter with the dolls' clothes, am now a middle-aged woman who makes Hearthstrings and grows cosmos too. This spring, my daughter began her first garden on a shoe-string budget. After the hoe and the trowel, she bought seeds for vegetables and seeds for pink and white cosmos. She never knew her great-grandmother's garden, but the connection is cosmic, unexplainable. It is what the best of life is made of—one small bridge that takes you back and gives you roots to grow on.

NATURAL ARTICHOKES AND POMEGRANATES

Making a Hearthstring of dried artichokes, pomegranates, and bay is like bottling up a little California sunshine and putting it on a string. The garnet shade of the pomegranates and the color of the artichoke's spiky petals contrast nicely. When dried, artichokes change color from fresh green with pale purple striations to a likeable earthy greenish-brown or brownish-green, depending on the success of the drying process and on your own ability to see things in their best light! Whether you see them green or see them brown, dried artichokes carry the natural colors of the earth and of growing things.

If you are a Californian or a Texan, you have a better choice of fresh greenery available than do others. Gertrude Stein told us that rose is a rose is a rose, but bay is a bay is a bay does not hold true! To all herb gardeners, there is only one bay—sweet bay (*Laurus nobilis*), a Mediterranean shrub usually grown in a container, set out in summer, and wintered indoors in all but the mildest climates.

The California bay tree is *Umbellaria californica*, an aromatic evergreen tree with glossy leaves and a pungent flavor, which has long been used for cooking in place of the slower-growing sweet bay. A fresh bay wreath ordered from California at Christmas will give you seasoning to use all year; it will be California bay.

Plantsmen will jump in at this point to make a strong case for always using Latin botanical names, so bay will not mean some-

Sweet Bay   *California Bay*   *Texas Bay*

INSTRUCTIONS FOR DRILLING POMEGRANATES

1. Buy an electric drill, either a standard plug-in type or one of the new cordless models, and a library of drill bits. Sizes $\frac{1}{16}$, $\frac{3}{32}$, and $\frac{5}{64}$ are readily available at hardware stores and the cost is a few dollars for each. Together they will allow you to drill not only pomegranates but nuts, spices, cones, and any other natural materials for stringing.

2. You will need to read the instruction booklet that comes with your drill to learn to operate the key that opens and closes the gripping mechanism that allows you to insert or remove the bits. A few turns of the key either way accomplishes this task.

3. Set up a work station and plug in your drill. Holding a pomegranate steady against an old cutting board with your thumb and forefinger, use the other hand to pull the trigger and drill into the pomegranate through to the surface of the board. Vary the angles at which you drill the fruit—top to bottom or side to side—for naturalness when you begin to string. Although the debris that is generated from drilling is mostly of a powdery nature, it couldn't hurt to wear protective goggles while drilling.

thing entirely different in California from what it means in Texas, or in a botanical garden in either place. While people often look at botanical names as an affectation and are impatient learning them, they are a great help even to novice gardeners once a few basics are absorbed. O, the confusion of common names! It goes on forever.

Texas bay, then, is red bay (*Persea borbonia*), a native shrub found along the Gulf Coast and traditionally used in that area for flavoring soups and meats in the same way that other bays are used. In fact, all three bays are entirely different plants that share a common name and can be used fresh or dried for seasoning or stringing. For Hearthstrings, use whichever fresh bay is available to you, or head back to the spice cupboard for the dried bay leaves most kitchens almost always have handy.

Y O U   N E E D

to make one 36-inch Hearthstring

6–8 dried pomegranates, about 3″ inches in diameter
Electric drill with a ³⁄₃₂-inch bit
Wooden cutting board
6–8 dried small artichokes
½ pound (about 300) fresh or dried bay leaves
Tapestry needle with a large eye
44 inches strong thin twine

T O   A S S E M B L E

Drill the pomegranates through from end to end on the cutting-board surface as instructed on page 26. Artichokes do not require drilling.

If you are using fresh bay leaves, strip the leaves from the branches and discard stems.

Thread the needle with the twine and tie a loop at the other end. Push the needle through the center of a bay leaf and slide it to the end of the string. Repeat this step with a few more bay leaves until you have the desired quantity. Then push the needle through the center of an artichoke at its widest point or through the drilled hole in the pomegranate and push to the end. Establish the pattern of your choice—the picture shows 2 inches of bay leaves followed by an artichoke, then 2 inches of bay leaves followed by a pomegranate—and follow it until the end. To end, remove the needle, tie another loop, and knot securely.

Remembering

My cheerful friend Chris Utterback is a master gardener who discovers and delights in new finds. One scorching summer day, she drove a hundred miles to a famous greenhouse in search of an unusual chocolate-scented cosmos (Cosmos astrosanguineus). Being the generous-hearted person she is, she bought one for me, too, when I was feeling under the weather. Up to my house pulled Chris's compact white wagon and out she popped—successful in her search, cosmos in hand, beaming as triumphantly as if she'd returned from botanizing in the Amazon. The day felt like the Amazon too, but Chris made the day!

Her home is a log house—not a cabin—filled with collections from the Southwest, including Indian baskets and Navajo rugs. Her taste is eclectic and she enjoys the purely whimsical. Who else would clearly see sculptural magic in a well-played tuba!

On the big fieldstone fireplace she has hung vertically, all parallel, three of her own Hearthstrings of artichokes and dried pomegranates. Big loopy bows of pale natural raffia are tied at each end in an informal way, a good choice for the desert colors of the room.

Chris's imagination is a mile wide. Her kitchen windowsills have boxes planted with a little forest of aloes, and, above them, in lieu of curtains spoiling her view of the meadow, she has swagged still another group of Hearthstrings.

KITCHEN SPICES

*T*hough passing fancies come and go, good scents are always in style. Not so many years ago, imaginative potpourris and delicately scented candles were introduced into the marketplace. They created a new awareness of the pleasure fragrance brings to our lives, not only on our bodies but throughout our homes. A new phrase was coined—"home fragrance."

Some scents, especially kitchen herbs and spices, are old familiars. These scents are zesty and energizing. We welcome them as a stimulating wake-me-up over the first sips of our morning coffee. We don't even have to be part of a new wave of homebodies to find it hard to resist hints of nutmeg, ginger, and cinnamon in our kitchens. Some of us remember the enticing aroma of grape jelly flavored with cinnamon sticks simmering on the stove.

Now you can make good-smelling spice strings to bring those same good scents back to your kitchen. If you hang several spice strings where the warmth and moisture of everyday cooking will draw out their powerful essential oils, you and your guests can enjoy the scent continually.

At greengrocers in the city we are used to see-ing fresh ginger rhizomes, and we commonly use its powdered form for seasoning Thanksgiving pies. Whole dried ginger root is less familiar.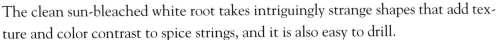
The clean sun-bleached white root takes intriguingly strange shapes that add tex-ture and color contrast to spice strings, and it is also easy to drill.

You need

to make one 36-inch Hearthstring

6 cinnamon sticks, each 4–6 inches long

6 large whole dried ginger roots

12 whole nutmeg

Electric drill with a 5/64-inch bit

Wooden cutting board

½ pound (about 300) fresh or dried bay leaves

Tapestry needle with a large eye

44 inches strong thin twine

To assemble

Drill the spices through on the cutting-board surface as directed on page 32. If you are using fresh bay leaves, strip the leaves from the branches and discard the stems.

Thread the needle with the twine and make a loop at the other end. Push the needle through the center of a bay leaf and slide it to the end of the string. Repeat this step with more bay leaves until you have a section 2 inches long. Push the needle through the hole in a cinnamon stick, then repeat the 2-

INSTRUCTIONS FOR DRILLING
SPICES AND NUTS

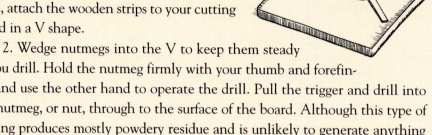

1. To drill nutmegs or nuts, obtain 2 pieces of wood about ½ inch high and 3 inches long from a lumberyard or hardware store. Narrow molding strips work well. Using a hammer and 1-inch-long nails, attach the wooden strips to your cutting board in a V shape.

2. Wedge nutmegs into the V to keep them steady as you drill. Hold the nutmeg firmly with your thumb and forefinger and use the other hand to operate the drill. Pull the trigger and drill into the nutmeg, or nut, through to the surface of the board. Although this type of drilling produces mostly powdery residue and is unlikely to generate anything of a trajectory nature, it never hurts to be overly cautious when it comes to your eyes, and some may prefer to wear protective goggles.

3. To drill ginger, hold the root firmly with your thumb and forefinger and use the other hand to operate the drill. Pull the trigger and drill into the center of the ginger through to the surface of the board.

4. The scent of cinnamon sticks is always a favorite, but drilling them requires time and patience. Cinnamon sticks are brittle, so they split and break off easily. A wise friend once cautioned, "Don't help the drill. Let it do its own work." That is the secret. Just the slightest bit of bearing down to "help" the drill is when the annoying break comes, so have patience and just hold the drill steady while it works. Don't try to hurry it along. As you would with nuts and other spices, hold the cinnamon stick steady against an old cutting board with your thumb and forefinger and use the other hand to operate the drill. Pull the trigger and drill into the center of the cinnamon stick to the surface of the board.

inch bay leaf section. Add a nutmeg, a ginger, and another nutmeg, then return to the bay leaves. Add another cinnamon stick and repeat the pattern until you reach 36 inches, ending with bay. To end, remove the needle, tie another loop, and knot securely.

Remembering

There are friends you don't see often but they are nonetheless lifelong friends.

Emily Santimauro lives in New Jersey, far away from me. She and John live a busy life gardening and spoiling their beloved grandchildren as often as they can. Every now and then she sends a letter. Once she wrote that years ago, when we met at the Bedford Antique Show and talked of herbs and homespuns, blue painted churns, old weaver's scarus, and red pomegranates, it was love at first sight! Instantly, we were friends.

Lucile Howard, a tall, elegant Bostonian, was the school librarian at the rural school where I taught when I was fresh from college and a new bride. After Walter and I bought a shingled cottage nestled in laurel woods, Lucile showed me how to start my first garden. She assured me I would enjoy caring for a garden and meeting other gardeners. She said, "Gardeners are the nicest people." There is an instant bond between people who enjoy helping things grow. Lucile also told me years ago, "You can't buy friendship with gifts, but little presents help to keep it alive!"

Sometimes, Emily sends little presents, like her famous "End of the Garden" pickles. One year, her Christmas basket contained pumpkin jam and tart red pomegranate jelly to serve with hot popovers for Christmas breakfast.

Just like Lucile, Emily knows that little presents, especially if they are homemade, help to keep friendship alive.

HARVEST CORN AND BAY

*B*right Indian corn is sold from giant wooden bins in front of farmstands here in New England in October. By then, a killing frost has ended another gardening year, and the appearance of Indian corn marks the beginning of a new season. The harvest corn shares many colors with sugar maples, aflame with color at that time of year. Russets, mahogany, brick, ivory, and vivid yellow brighten each ear of corn, making it hard to select favorites. Each one seems to be the best one yet. You rummage through the bins from top to bottom, but it is like berry picking in summer: Each strawberry or blueberry is just slightly more perfect to your eye than the one just before. Usually the corn husks are yellow-ivory, but sometimes they are marked with purple or burgundy. Though you will not be using the husks for this project, when they are colorful, choosing is all the harder.

To make this Hearthstring, you must select a few colorful ears of harvest corn then saw the ears into chunks. An electric saw bounces off the hard corn kernels and does not work, but a sharp hand saw does the job quickly. The chunks of corn may need to be drilled for stringing after they are cut; if so, drill through the pithy center as you hold the chunk of corn on end with your hand.

In keeping with the rustic charm of this Hearthstring, try using rough sisal or farmers' baling twine to form bows at each end when you have finished. Hang one string on the back of your kitchen door, or make up several lengths and use them to decorate the Thanksgiving table.

YOU NEED
to make one 36-inch Hearthstring

2–3 ears brightly colored Indian corn
Sharp hand saw

Wood cutting board
½ pound (about 300) fresh or dried bay leaves
44 inches strong thin twine
Tapestry needle with a large eye
2 yards sisal twine

To assemble

Using a sharp hand saw on a cutting-board surface, saw each ear of corn into 1½-inch chunks. You may want to discard the end tips, as they are not as attractive.

If using fresh bay leaves, strip leaves from the branches and discard stems.

Thread the needle with the twine and make a loop at the other end. Push the needle through the center of a bay leaf and slide it to the end of the string. Repeat this step with more bay leaves until you have a section 1 inch long.

Push the needle through the center of a chunk of corn and slide it next to the bay leaves. Follow with another chunk of corn. Follow the pattern of 1 inch of bay leaves alternating with chunks of corn to the end, making sure to end with bay. Remove the needle, tie another loop, and knot securely.

Cut the sisal twine in half, then cut 6 inches from each half. Form each of the longer lengths into a loopy bow by wrapping the twine back and forth between your thumb and little finger in a figure 8. Tie each bow in the middle with the short length of twine, then attach to either end of the finished string, leaving the loops free.

Remembering

When fall comes in New England, there is an irresistible urge to mark the season with decoration and celebration. Marya and Jim Martinell generously share their sense of fun. They begin weeks ahead, visiting nearby farms to select only perfect giant pumpkins, then they store them in the tool shed for the remainder of October. The night before Halloween, they host a carving party.

On the Big Night, when the spooks are out and the witches take to their brooms, dozens of lighted pumpkins with whimsical, even downright comical, faces are set out on the lawn in front of Jim's veterinary hospital on Main Street. Most of their small-town neighbors come by to see the sight. Jim is on hand to welcome the friendly crowd, and that night the traffic goes by the front of the place at a snail's pace.

Even if you were carrying the burdens of Atlas squarely on your shoulders, you couldn't drive by that display of Jack O'Lanterns without feeling happy at the sight. It's a real happening that touches the child within us all.

DELLA ROBBIA

*L*ush! Lavish! Totally extravagant! This Della Robbia string is the ultimate fantasy of fruit, nuts, cones, tiny vegetables, and glossy leaves, as elegant as if it came from the workshops of the Florentine masters. Three generations of the Della Robbia family worked in Florence as sculptors and craftsmen in the fifteenth and sixteenth centuries. In the great churches of Renaissance Italy, their carved reliefs of enamel-glazed terra-cotta fruits and flowers, nuts and wheat bordered and framed Madonnas and nativity scenes. Today, the name Della Robbia is often used to mean an arrangement of bountiful fruits used for decoration.

Taking its inspiration from the style of the Florentines, your own garland can be absolutely state-of-the-art, using some of the exciting new freeze-dried fruits and vegetables now available (see page 100 for mail-order sources). The pioneers of the freeze-drying process have invested large sums in their equipment and can deliver almost anything your heart desires, from slices of melon to stalks of asparagus—at a price, of course. Nothing in the world of dried materials is as sensational or as costly as freeze-drying, since the process is still in its infancy. Each batch of fruits or flowers requires several days in a small vacuum chamber to completely extract moisture from the product. Freeze drying is serious business, not possible at home.

To keep these astoundingly true-to-nature dried materials at their best, they must be carefully sheltered from light and humidity. Their initial cost demands that they be treated with respect, and their very fragile nature requires assiduous care.

What is available? Baby red potatoes, mushrooms, small whole pears, yam slices, quail eggs, scallions, gardenias, and hyacinth bulbs, complete with blossoms and root systems intact. You can let your imagination go as far as your purse will allow, incorporating lots of freeze-drieds or only a few.

Whatever fruits and flora you select, try salal, or, as they are popularly called,

lemon leaves, for this garland. Lemon leaves are glossy and larger in proportion to the fruits than bay leaves. If too large, the lemon leaves can be pleated into double or triple folds as you string them. Salal grows in the Pacific Northwest and is sold throughout the country in flower shops. You should have no trouble finding it in stock or ordering a bunch through your florist, even in small towns. These leaves are so pretty to look at, you may decide to use longer sections of leaves and less of the freeze-dried fruits for a different but equally pretty Della Robbia string.

Y O U   N E E D

to make one 36-inch Hearthstring

6 or more large Brazil nuts or walnuts
Electric drill with ³⁄₃₂-inch bit
Wooden cutting board
1 bunch (about 300) fresh lemon leaves
Tapestry needle with a large eye
44 inches strong thin twine
6 freeze-dried strawberries
3 freeze-dried asparagus stalks
3 or more large cones, such as those from a red pine tree
6 freeze-dried mushrooms
2 yards red velvet ribbon, ¼–½-inch wide

T O   A S S E M B L E

Drill the nuts on a cutting-board surface as directed on page 32. Strip the lemon leaves from the branches and discard stems.

Thread the needle with the twine and tie a loop at the other end. Fold a lemon leaf in half horizontally, veins and stem inward, and push the needle through the center of the leaf, piercing both halves. Slide leaf to the end of the string. Repeat with 4–5 more leaves. Then push the needle through two strawberries and slide them next to the leaves. Push the needle through an asparagus stalk, then 4–5 leaves, a pine cone, then 4–5 leaves, two mushrooms, then 4–5 leaves, then two nuts, followed by 4–5 leaves, sliding each to the end of the string. Repeat this pattern—or any other eye-pleasing combination you choose—to the end of the string, making sure to finish with leaves.

To end, remove needle, form another loop, and knot securely.

Cut the ribbon into 2 pieces, each one yard long. Tie to the finished string at each end after the last section of leaves, and form a bow as though you were tying a shoelace, leaving the loops free.

Regional Specialties

NEW ENGLAND CRANBERRY BEANS

Often, a feeling of amazement comes over us when events come together in unexpected ways. It's a feeling we've all had. In the end, small coincidences must be regarded as things coming full circle in some unexplainable fashion. For example, old recipes and seed lists as well as folklore tell us about the virtues of cranberry beans. Then scientists and researchers shuffle around the old food groups, lessening emphasis on meats and fats and heaping new paeans of praise on the humble bean!

For its economy and as a source of fiber and protein the bean is without equal. Of course, that brings things full circle, because the bean was a family favorite from colonial times in America through the years of the Great Depression. Many of our grandmothers baked an earthenware pot of beans and steamed a loaf of brown bread as a standard part of their weekly fare. In small towns, countless bean suppers with crispy slaw and melt-in-the-mouth homemade pies have made local cooks famous and kept churches solvent, with their roofs repaired and their heating bills paid.

One New England lady, Margery Thoresen, who grew up in the town of Lexington, Massachusetts, where the Minutemen fought the first battle of the Revolution, recalls her mother drying beans. On the third floor of their old homestead, newspapers were spread out and beans were put down to dry for winter baking. She remembers that they were Kentucky Wonder, a kind of green pole bean commonly grown today for its tenderness. But to dry? Sure enough, another of those full circles! The spirited and sensible garden writer Eleanor Perenyi confirms that she does exactly the same thing with Kentucky Wonders. In fact, she wonders why people don't dry the more mature beans when the crop gets ahead of them.

> ### GREAT BEANS TO GROW FOR DECORATION
> ### (even if you'll never eat one!)
>
> *Vermont Cranberry Pole Beans*
> (mottled red pods, good for stringing)
>
> *Scarlet Runner Pole Beans*
> (scarlet flowers all summer)
>
> *White Knight Runner Pole Beans*
> (white blossoms all summer)
>
> *Ornamental Hyacinth Beans*
> (lavender blossoms all summer)

Cranberry beans are shell beans with a mottled red and white pod. They are an old-fashioned variety still valued for their succulent flavor. In Kentucky and Tennessee, these beans were strung by the hearth for winter supplies and the dried beans were called Leather Breeches. As they dry, the color dims somewhat. But the bean strings have a great harvest look, and combine well with apple strings for decoration in an old-fashioned kitchen.

YOU NEED

to make one 24-inch Hearthstring

50 (about 1½ pounds) fresh cranberry bean pods
Tapestry needle with a large eye
38 inches strong thin twine

HEARTHSTRINGS

44

Thread the needle with the twine and tie a loop at the other end. Gently push the needle through the biggest (top) part of a bean and slide it to the end of the string. Follow with another bean and arrange it so that the end points in the opposite direction from the previous bean. Repeat until your string of beans reaches 30 inches. (The beans will shrink as they dry, making the string only 24 inches long after they've dried.) To end, remove the needle, tie another loop, and knot securely.

After the string is dry, about a week later, ease the pods together gently and shorten the string. Then tie yet another loop, knot in place, and clip off unneeded length of twine to finish your project.

BEANS! BEAUTIFUL BEANS!

Even if you resist the new cult of meatless menus with beans and rice, bulgur and lentils as mealtime stars, you might want to grow beans on poles or trellises simply for their beauty. Pole beans can be thought of as fast and easy to grow annual vines. Carefully selected varieties can provide sensational color to screen off a work area, like your compost pile or a storage shed. In England, far more often than in America, beans are brush-staked and grown in kitchen gardens ornamentally as much as for food. Now, as we learn to combine vegetables, herbs, and flowers in the *potager* style, delicious scarlet runner beans and ornamental lavender-flowered hyacinth beans are finding new fans. Try some in places you have planted morning glories in the past and enjoy a new adventure in gardening.

PORK AND BEANS

Pick over carefully a quart of beans and let them soak overnight. In the morning wash and drain in another water and put on to boil in cold water with half teaspoon of soda. Let them come to a boil then drain again. Cover with cold water once more and boil them 15 minutes, or until the skin of the beans will crack when taken out and blown upon. Drain the beans again, put them into an earthen beanpot, adding 1 tablespoon of salt and 3 tablespoons of molasses, cover with hot water, place in the center 1 lb. of salt pork, first scalding it with hot water and scoring the rind across the top ¼ inch apart to indicate where the slices are to be cut. Place the pot in the oven and bake six hours or longer. Keep the oven at moderate heat, add hot water from the teakettle as needed on account of evaporation, to keep the beans moist. Keep the pot covered so the beans will not burn on top.

Sunshine Cook Book
A Collection of Valuable Recipes and
Menus Gathered from Various Sources
Mrs. Jennie E. Underhill
New London, Conn.
1910

OHIO BUCKEYES

Ohio is a much maligned state! People say "Ohio" with such a ho-hum way about them. No one ever says, "I'm going to Ohio for my summer vacation." So this is a song in praise of Ohio. First, there are the lakes—huge and small. And, in Holmes County, where the Amish live, the woods are filled with trillium in springtime, and buggies are tied up at the general store in towns with appealing names like Sugar Creek. And long ago, Johnny Appleseed sowed the seeds that

made Ohio apple country a glorious place to visit during apple blossom season and in the fall.

Of course, Ohio is the Buckeye State, and its people are affectionately called buckeyes. But the true Ohio buckeye (*Aesculus glabra*) is a tree of the horse-chestnut family that grows up to 30 feet tall and blooms in May with pale yellow-green flowers. The fruit of the buckeye tree that we use for this project resembles a hazelnut or filbert, a tawny brown nut that is lighter at each end than it is in the middle. In the fall, Ohio farmers sell baskets of them at farmer's markets and some Ohioans can gather them in their own backyards. If you live far from a buckeye tree, you can substitute hazelnuts or filberts for nearly the same effect. It is best to drill them for making Hearthstrings, though it is not impossible to push a sharp needle through with persistence.

YOU NEED

to make one 40-inch Hearthstring

About 45 Ohio buckeyes
Electric drill with a 5/64-inch bit
Wooden cutting board
Tapestry needle with a large eye
88 inches strong, thin, light-colored twine

TO ASSEMBLE

Drill the buckeyes through from end to end on a cutting-board surface as directed on page 32.

Thread the needle with the twine and tie a knot at the other end. As an interesting variation, try forming a knot in the twine between each buckeye, giving the same effect as individual beads in a necklace. To do this, first push the needle through the hole in a buckeye and slide the nut to the end of the string. Make a loop

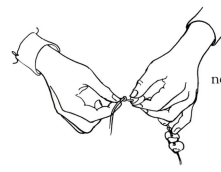

with the twine and slide the needle through to make the decorative knot. Repeat until all the buckeyes are strung. To end, remove the needle, tie another loop, and knot firmly.

Remembering

On the weekends, Hope and John Richardson retreat from their house in the city to an unpainted weathered clapboard cabin in a rural area of southern Ohio. John's grandfather lived on this farm and John knew it as a boy. Though his career has taken him many places, John seems happy right here. Clearly, it is a place of contentment.

Now it is a Christmas-tree farm, where families come to cut the tall, well-shaped trees John has grown with pride. When they leave with a tree, perhaps those shoppers also take home a sense of the beauty of the hilly southern Ohio landscape. On the farm there is a pond, and in the fall and winter wild scarlet rose hips flourish at the edge of the woods beside the bristly wild teasels.

Hope grows and writes about herbs. In fact, we met on a tour of herb gardens in Scotland. Her writing and her gardens share a sense of poetry and attention to detail. There is an early spring kitchen garden, but that is just the beginning. Vegetables and herbs are harvested until the late October frost warning. Then a cover crop of "green manure" is sown—so sensible and so seldom done by home gardeners.

Like all really good gardens, this one is intensely personal. There is a bed planted in tribute to a heroic Civil War ancestor—there's that poetry and pride again. The garden includes unusual plants like skirret (Sium sisarum), a carrot-family herb used as a vegetable in Saxon England. Nearby grows one of the newest herb cultivars, the nearly hardy rosemary called Arp.

No one could take the ride along this road so far off the beaten path, spot the front porch of this proud little cabin, a place where nothing shatters the peace, and not be touched by the aura of quiet contentment.

SOUTHWEST CHILIES

The Southwest style has stolen hearts all over America. Native American silver with western jeans and handsome boots are as likely to be worn in New England as in Santa Fe or Tucson. You still have to go west for authentic green chili dishes or beef sun-dried on the roof tops, but Tex-Mex cuisine has invaded the popular culture. Though Indian curries and some regional specialties of Provence make hot red peppers staples in other parts of the world, fiery red strings of chilies are most common in the American Southwest. Traditional *ristras* are strung up in the fall, then hung to dry in the desert air. As more southwestern touches come to home decorating, *ristras* are growing in popularity.

Like their cousins bell peppers and long sweet frying peppers, chilies are members of the capsicum family, natives of South America. Many varieties of pep-

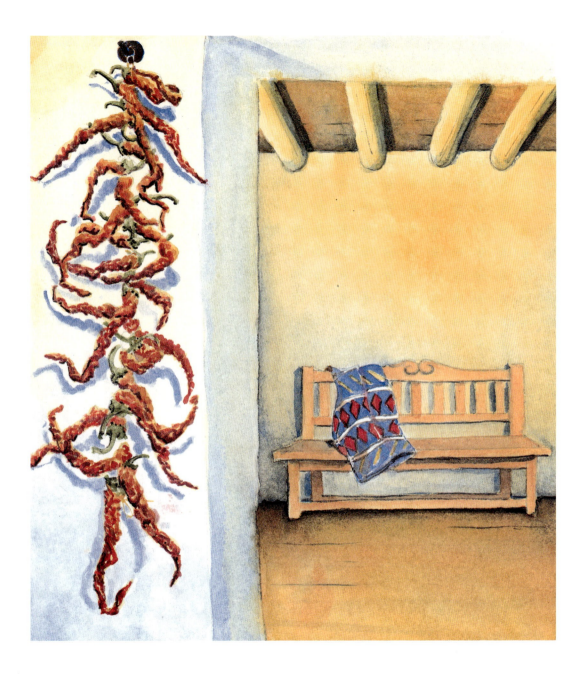

pers are offered in seed catalogues. They are easy to grow, though they are frost sensitive. Start seedlings indoors in cold climates, then line them out in the garden after all danger of frost has passed. Give the soil time to warm up. Later on, toward the end of the growing season, when the cold nights begin, gather all green chili peppers remaining on the plants. Spread them out on newspapers in a warm, dry place with good air circulation to prevent spoilage. The color will change from green to red. Then the peppers are ready to string.

The inner ribs and seeds are the hottest part of the peppers, but you will still want to wear gloves and work outdoors in fresh air to eliminate sneezes. Traditional *ristras* require many pounds of chilies to knot and braid. This Hearthstring is simpler—quick and easy to do.

YOU NEED
to make one 24-inch Hearthstring

Tapestry needle with a large eye
32 inches heavy-duty sewing thread or fishing line
About 50 fresh or dried cayenne or other thin-skinned peppers

TO ASSEMBLE

Thread your needle and tie a loop at the other end. Pierce a chili pepper with the needle just below the green stem, into the top of the full round flesh of the pepper, and slide it to the end of the string. Repeat until all peppers are strung.

To end, remove the needle, tie another loop, and knot firmly. If you plan to hang this string vertically, like a traditional *ristra*, omit the ending loop and just knot firmly.

Strings for the Christmas Tree

CARDAMOM SEEDS

Reading that cardamom (*Elettaria cardamomum*) is a spice of the ginger family invariably leads to the question: What is the difference between an herb and a spice? It is a point of continual speculation. The problem isn't helped when both terms are used interchangeably with the word "seasoning." The whole picture becomes cloudy not only botanically but linguistically as well. To clear the fog somewhat, a useful clarification is found in Frederick Rosengarten's 1969 *The Book of Spices:* "Generally speaking, when the aromatic or fragrant vegetable product used to flavor food or beverage is from plants of tropical origin, it is considered a spice; when from plants of temperate regions, it may be considered a culinary herb."

Cloudy issues concerning cardamom come up again. When grown as a crop for the spice trade, cardamom is found strictly in the tropics, but in our part of the world it is often seen as a fast-growing house plant. The leaves are pungent and spicy, yet it is not the leaves that are used for seasoning, it is the seeds.

Still more confusion comes into the cardamom story. Both natural green and bleached white cardamom pods are sold as cardamom seed. Actually, it is the tiny dark seeds within these outer pods that are crushed for seasoning. For making

Hearthstrings, however, the pods are the thing! You can use either green or white—green cardamom seeds are easier to find and less expensive. These pods are easy to pierce with a thin, sharp needle, but because they are very small, it takes some patience to build up a string. You only have to do the job once, because a cardamom-seed string lasts for years. You might want to swag one around your spice shelf or along a kitchen cupboard during the winter holidays. Their size makes them perfect garlands for charming tabletop feather trees or for bare branches stuck into an old country crock.

Widely known in India for its use in blending curries, in the Middle East for flavoring coffee, and in Scandinavia for yeast breads and Christmas cookies, cardamom is scarcely known in America. An advertising slogan says: "If you've never seen it, it's new to you!" For many of us, that's just how it is with cardamom, so get acquainted.

You need
to make one 60-inch Hearthstring

Thin sewing needle with a large eye and sharp point
68 inches strong sewing thread or nylon fishing line
3 ounces (about 250) whole green or white cardamom seed pods

To assemble

Thread your needle and tie a loop at the other end. Gently stab the needle through the center of a seed pod and slide it to the end of the string. Repeat until you have used all seed pods.

To end, remove the needle, tie another loop, and knot securely.

STRINGS FOR THE CHRISTMAS TREE

ORANGE SLICES AND BAY

As much as the scent of evergreens and spices, the scent of oranges is an enticing part of the Christmas season. Citrus scents are not only fresh, light, and easy to live with, they are traditionally associated with the holiday season. Since citrus fruits were exotics in England and colonial America, they were imported at great cost or grown in wood-fire-heated hothouses by the very rich. George Washington grew oranges in a glass house, called the Orangerie, at Mount Vernon. Even as late as a generation ago, oranges were a great treat to be had only at Christmas for many families. Our mothers and grandmothers remember the excitement of having an orange in their Christmas stockings.

This Hearthstrings project uses dried orange slices strung with bay, which is also one of the herbs long associated with Christmas. Drying orange slices is so delightfully simple to do! Small, thin-skinned oranges are best to use: thick-skinned oranges will spoil easily. They are easily dried at home in the oven at very low heat, or in an electric dehydrator. Keeping the heat low cannot be stressed enough. Low heat ensures that they retain their lovely citrus fragrance as well as their best color.

You will be enchanted by the translucent magic of dried orange slices! Remember to dry extra slices for the Christmas tree. String them on ordinary white sewing thread, and the light will shine through, creating a soft, lovely effect. The heat of the tree lights will also draw out the essential oils in the oranges, filling the room with their scent.

to make one 36-inch Hearthstring

6 small thin-skinned oranges, about 3 inches in diameter
Sharp paring knife
Cookie sheet and slow oven
½ pound (about 300) fresh or dried bay leaves
Tapestry needle with a large eye
44 inches strong thin twine

To assemble

Cut the oranges horizontally with the paring knife into 5 slices, not including the end pieces of rind, which should be discarded. Arrange in a single layer on a cookie sheet and place in an oven set at 200°F or less. This will take about 2 hours. Keep an eye on them and remove as soon as they feel leathery, not brittle, to the touch. If using fresh bay leaves, strip the leaves from the branches and discard stems.

Thread the needle with the twine and tie a loop at the other end. Gently push the needle through a bay leaf and slide it to the end of the string. Follow with another leaf until you have about 2 inches of leaves. Then push the needle through the center of an orange slice and slide it next to the bay leaves. Follow with more orange slices until you have established a pattern of 2 inches of leaves followed by 2 inches of oranges. Always begin and end with leaves. When you have reached the 36-inch length, remove needle, tie another loop in the twine, then knot securely.

RED ROSE HIPS

Generations ago, roses were planted near cellar entrances and in shady cemeteries. Later, popular taste favored modern hybrid tea roses and many species of fragrant older roses nearly fell into extinction. Only a few small nurseries propagated old-fashioned shrub roses, so they were hard to find. Some dedicated rose lovers searched the countryside to find robust survivors of these forgotten varieties. The survivors were properly identified and gradually returned to the lists of the bigger commercial growers. Thanks to the efforts of these persistent rosarians, old roses with their romantic names are now available from big mail-order nurseries and even small neighborhood garden centers.

In part, new editions of the writings of Vita Sackville-West reawakened interest in old roses. She wrote with enthusiasm about her own love of shrub roses. American readers and magazine photographers flocked to her gardens at Sissinghurst in Kent. There, she and her husband, Harold Nicolson, had trained old roses along wires to create natural barriers and set them rambling through the trees.

Old-fashioned shrub roses require more space than modern tea roses and generally provide shorter periods of bloom. On the other hand, shrub roses offer richer fragrances and many species offer a burst of color in autumn with their brilliant hips. Many gardeners enjoy the hips as much as the blossoms. Some rose hips, bright berries full of seeds, are deep red, almost black. Some are scarlet, some are crimson. Some species produce their hips in late summer, others in the fall. By winter the birds have feasted on them and most hips are gone.

The dog roses (*Rosa canina*) that run wild have small hips that remain green until frost, when they magically turn scarlet. They are perfect for flower arrangements and, dried, in wreaths for winter, but they are too small for stringing. Rugged rugosa roses produce large fat hips nearly the size of small cherry tomatoes. It is tempting to gather them to string, but all experiments have proved useless and unpleasant because the hips became wormy.

So, for Hearthstrings, commercially dried rose hips, very reasonable in cost, are a must. They are uniformly round and bright. When they are strung, they look similar to cranberries. If they are carefully stored in a place where mice won't be lured to a nutritious snack, rose-hip strings will last for several years.

If you sit down to make a rose-hip chain, perhaps you'll buy some extra rose hips for tea so you can sip as you work. The tea has a tart citrus taste and is a good source of vitamin C. Make it by crushing a few of the dried hips and putting them in a tea ball as you would any loose tea. It is especially delicious when sweetened with honey.

To make this Hearthstring, you will need a thin needle with a very sharp point. It is slow work, but when you finish, the string will be bright, cheerful, long-lasting, and inexpensive, so it is worth the effort. You'll be pleased with the results.

You need
to make one 36-inch Hearthstring

Thin needle with a sharp point
44 inches strong sewing thread
3 ounces (about 100) whole dried rose hips

To assemble

Thread your needle and tie a loop at the opposite end. Holding a rose hip against a hard, flat surface, *firmly* push the needle through the center of the fruit and slide it to the end of the string. The hips do require some pressure to pierce. Repeat until all hips are strung.

When you have finished your string, remove the needle, tie another loop, and knot securely.

GOLDEN RAISINS

*P*ennsylvanians have extremely rich folk traditions and work hard to record and preserve them. Carpet weavers and redware potters today work in the same manner as their early counterparts. Oral history projects have documented all sorts of crafts, from rye-grass basketmakers to farm ladies who use herbs and garden vegetables to dye Easter eggs. Antique collectors hunt for old handmade Christmas decorations in the state where the Christmas tree made its first appearance in America. Historian Alfred L. Schoemaker searched through newspaper records and journals while compiling data for his book, *Christmas in Pennsylvania*, in which he cites an 1857 account of a tree decorated with raisin chains. So we know this Hearthstrings project comes out of a truly old Pennsylvania tradition, though one less well known than popcorn or cranberry chains. Mellow color and diminutive size give raisin strings great charm.

Strings can be made of dark sun-dried California raisins or golden raisins, or in imaginative patterns alternating and combining both. No matter what color you use, the raisins will become sticky with handling, and so will your fingers, before you get too far along in the string. In fact, you'll wonder how you ever got into this unless you freeze the raisins before you begin. Remove only enough raisins from the freezer to complete a yard at a time. If wrapped and stored in the freezer, your raisin strings can be used again and again for years.

to make one 3-yard Hearthstring

1 10-ounce box golden raisins
Thin needle with a large eye and sharp point
116 inches nylon fishing line or strong sewing thread

TO ASSEMBLE

Freeze raisins overnight, then remove from the freezer only what you will be using for a yard at a time—about 65 raisins, so call it a handful.

Thread the needle with the fishing line or thread and tie a loop at the opposite end. Push the needle through the center of a raisin and slide it to the opposite end of the string. Repeat until you've strung a yard of raisins, then get another handful out of the freezer. Repeat until all raisins are strung.

To end, remove the needle, tie another loop, and knot securely.

GILDED NUTS

*T*welfth Night, Epiphany, or "Little Christmas" is the Christian feast marking the day when the Wise Men arrived at Bethlehem with their gifts of gold, frankincense, and myrrh. In Europe, January 6 is still the time when families exchange gifts and gather in celebration of the winter holidays. Traditionally, the French celebrate the day with a cake into which a gold coin, now more often a foil-wrapped bean, has been baked. The reveler whose piece of cake contains the gold coin, a symbol of the gifts of the Wise Men, becomes King for the year.

Gilding natural things like nutmegs or sprigs of rosemary is another ancient holiday custom in honor of the gifts of the Magi. Gilded nut strings festooning the

fireplace or looped through bare branches as a centerpiece have a gracious traditional look perfect for the season.

Your own Twelfth Night celebration for family and friends can wind up the holidays in a charming, unexpected way. You can carry on the old tradition of the gold coin or bean in your party cake and use gilded nuts as your decorating theme. Certainly, gilded nuts can be used at any time during the holiday season, or even as an elegant decoration at another time of year, but Twelfth Night is a grand excuse!

Select nuts that are the right size and scale for your project. For example, do not use large walnuts or giant Brazil nuts for a small table tree. Combine many kinds of nuts, both large and small, in pleasing patterns for a long string on a large tree. Hard-shelled nuts must be drilled for stringing. They are easily drilled, except for Brazil nuts. Like cinnamon sticks, Brazil nuts teach a lesson in patience when they are drilled!

After Twelfth Night, wrap your gilded strings loosely in tissue and store in a cool, dry place to be used again next year.

Y OU NEED

to make one 36-inch Hearthstring

16 ounces mixed almonds, filberts, walnuts, and other nuts in their shells
Electric drill with a ⁵⁄₆₄-inch bit
Wooden cutting board
Dust mask and protective gloves
Shallow box
Gold metallic spray paint
Long sewing needle with a large eye
80 inches gold metallic cord

T O ASSEMBLE

Drill the nuts through from side to side on the cutting board as instructed on page 32.

HEARTHSTRINGS

Put on a dust mask to cover your nose and mouth and put gloves on your hands. Arrange the nuts in a single layer in the bottom of a shallow box. Bring the box outdoors and spray the nuts with gold paint. Allow to dry. Turn the nuts and paint the other side. Allow to dry.

Thread the needle with the gold cord and tie a loop at the other end.

Push the needle through the hole in a nut and slide it to the end of the string. Make a loop with the cord and slide the needle through to make a decorative knot. Establish a pattern of alternating nuts and knots, giving the same effect as individual beads on a necklace. It is prettier if the nuts are not too close together, allowing the cord to show. Repeat until all the nuts are strung. To end, remove the needle, tie another loop, and knot firmly.

MATHILDA'S SWISS CHRISTMAS BARS

Mathilda Stadler, my mother-in-law, was one of 13 children born to a farmer in the Appenzell region of Switzerland. This is one of her old family recipes.

Blend together 1 pound brown sugar and one-half pint sour cream. Melt and add ¼ cup butter.

Sift together 4 cups flour, 2 teaspoons baking powder, ¼ teaspoon salt, 2 teaspoons cinnamon, ½ teaspoon cloves, and ½ teaspoon nutmeg.

Combine sugar mixture and dry ingredients. Add 2 small jars candied citron and 1 cup finely chopped walnuts.

Spread on an ungreased cookie sheet and bake at 350°F for 30 minutes.

Frost while warm with a thin buttercream icing and slice into 1-inch squares. Keeps for several weeks in an airtight tin.

STRINGS FOR THE CHRISTMAS TREE

Decorative Country Strings

A WEAVER'S STRING

You needn't be a weaver to love the tools and the craftsmanship of handweaving. The Shakers were known for the efficiency and fine design of even their most functional objects, and their spinning wheels and weaving tools are no exception. Today's antiques collectors seek out both the large "walking wheels" used to spin woolen yarns and the smaller flax wheels. In fact, the popularity of spinning wheels, flax breakers, scarns, and hand-made shuttles and bobbins as collectibles illustrates the fascination many of us have with the creative process of weaving.

Handwoven rag rugs are as popular today as they were in colonial times, when each bit of fabric was so precious that clothes were recycled from oldest members of the family down the line to the youngest and made their last appearance in carpeting. For rag rug making, old garments were torn into long, narrow strips, then the strips were joined together and rolled into balls. These colorful balls—often made of old calicos and muslins in mellow colors and charming patterns—are among the domestic objects that give us kinship to women of the past, whom we admire because they often made what they needed with beauty and creativity. Simple early American furnishings can certainly be complemented by a Pennsylvania rye-grass basket filled with rag balls, colorful, warm, and homey.

You can make a few rag balls from one of your child's outgrown garments or one of your mother's hand-me-downs and start your own tradition with them. Join your rag balls with apples and spices to make a weaver's Hearthstring that is both new and old.

"The domestic arts are not stationary, but to a great extent the contributions are anonymous, and often remain private for a long time."

—*Shelly Karpilow*

YOU NEED

to make one 36-inch Hearthstring

1 old colorfully patterned garment, such as a shirt
12 whole nutmegs
12 short cinnamon sticks
Electric drill with a ¹⁄₁₆-inch bit
Wooden cutting board
Tapestry needle with a large eye
44 inches strong thin twine
40 slices dried red apples

TO ASSEMBLE

Tear garment lengthwise into ½-inch-wide strips—as many as needed to roll into a ball about 3 inches in diameter. Fold the first inch of fabric back away from you, then begin winding the remainder of the strip. Tuck in the ends or join them with a stitch. Roll the second strip in the same manner around the first strip. Repeat until you have made 4 balls.

Drill nutmegs and cinnamon sticks on the cutting-board surface as instructed on page 32.

Thread the needle with the twine and tie a loop at the other end. Push the needle through the center of a rag ball and slide it to the end of the string. Follow with 4–5 slices of dried apple, then a nutmeg, cinnamon stick, and another nutmeg. Add another rag ball and follow this pattern, or one of your own choosing, consistently to the end, making sure to finish with a rag ball.

To end, remove needle, tie another loop, and knot securely.

Remembering

Lori Lunn and her husband, Ron, live in a house in a meadow high in the Litchfield Hills of Connecticut. Their meadow slopes off behind the herb garden to a small pond. It's a sheltered place where bluebirds stay all winter and provide constant entertainment when watched from the keeping-room window. The house was built only a few years ago but looks so relaxed in its setting you could easily be fooled into thinking it is 200 years old. The authentic colonial front door and interior paneling were salvaged from an early house no longer standing.

Ron planned the Count Rumford–style fireplace. He keeps it going with many logs on a typical winter day, though it is Lori who adds the magic warmth to the house. She found the red stone quoin from Vermont, dated 1801, which sits to one side of the hearth, and the parade of woolly nineteenth-century toy sheep that marches across the mantelpiece. Just above the open fire she has hung several Hearthstrings. All of them are uniquely original combinations of bay leaves and natural things, made by two or three "Herb Ladies" whom she counts among her friends.

Another wee bit of a room off the kitchen, the butt'ry, is lined with shelves full of country crocks and pickles put up in old jars. There is a bird's nest or two from Lori's collection, and an early splint basket filled to the brim with hollowed-out quails' eggs. In the butt'ry there are more Hearthstrings, because this is a room meant for putting food by, as the old Yankee saying goes, so strings of foodstuffs hung in the old colonial way seem very much at home.

CINNAMON APPLE HEARTS AND STARS

*E*veryone loves to bake cut-out sugar cookies in all their tasty variations. The Swedish flavor theirs with cardamom and the Moravians use molasses and spicy ginger, then roll their dough paper thin.

In Pennsylvania, cookie baking has always been part of the holiday tradition. Long ago, tinsmiths in Pennsylvania made cookie cutters in fanciful animal shapes and the much-loved heart-in-hand pattern prized by antiques collectors, as well as imaginative hearts and stars. Tin cookie cutters are still being made and are every bit as loved and collected by present-day cookie bakers as they were generations ago.

To make a cinnamon heart and star string, you will need a very small cutter of each shape to cut apple slices into hearts and stars before drying. After cutting the shapes, you roll them in a "spice bath" of powdered spices such as allspice, cinnamon, cloves, nutmeg, and ginger, mixed and added to ground orris root. You can use whatever spices you have available to make your blend, not just those mentioned above. Be practical and inventive: Use the spices that have been on your pantry shelf longest, then replace them for fresh flavor when cooking. Though the

SPICE BALL POMANDERS

These spice balls were originally called maste balls, maste being the name for the pulp left over after jelly making. This recipe, using applesauce instead of maste, was developed by Frances Williams and passed along by Helen McBride, who were both honored members of the New England Unit of the Herb Society of America, founded in Boston more than 50 years ago.

½ cup applesauce
½ teaspoon powdered orris root
¾ cup mixed ground spices, such as allspice,
           cinnamon, cloves, ginger, mace, and
           nutmeg
20 whole cloves
10 or 20 strips of narrow ribbon, depending on
           size of balls, each 18 inches long

Mix together the applesauce, orris root, and spices until thoroughly blended. Divide mixture into 10 balls the size of a quarter or 20 balls the size of a dime. Insert a crochet hook through the center of each spice ball and draw the ribbon through. Anchor the ribbon with 2 whole cloves. Hang overnight to dry. Do *not* double the recipe.

list of spices is very flexible, don't get too far off the path and use curry or turmeric, for instance. Make sure the fragrances are compatible. As obvious as this may sound to some, it has proved to be a fatal mistake to others!

You must, however, use orris root as a fixative in your blend. It holds the spicy fragrance, so it lasts, and keeps the apple slices from shrinking substantially during the drying process.

Orris root comes from the Florentine iris, a species of *Iris germanica* with white blossoms that is beautiful and easy to grow in your herb garden. But drying and grinding up the root at home is needlessly laborious and messy. Fine quality ground orris root is inexpensive and easily obtainable. It is sometimes found at pharmacies and is always offered by herb shops and mail order catalogues. Store-bought orris root has been cured in the sun and aged properly to bring out its violet-like fragrance. It has clean color and pure quality.

YOU NEED

to make one 30-inch Hearthstring

4–5 medium fresh red or green apples

2–2½-inch heart-shaped cookie cutter

2–2½-inch star-shaped cookie cutter

¾ cup mixed cinnamon and assorted ground spices

½ teaspoon orris root

Sharp paring knife

8 whole nutmegs

Electric drill with a ¹⁄₁₆-inch bit

Wooden cutting board

4 ounces (about 75) fresh or dried bay leaves

Tapestry needle with a large eye

38 inches strong sewing thread or nylon fishing line

Using a sharp paring knife, trim top and bottom ends off each apple. Then slice apples horizontally into thin slices—about 4 or 5 slices per apple. Do not core. Using the cookie cutters, cut a star or a heart out of the center of each slice. Combine the mixed spices and orris root and roll cutouts quickly in this mixture. Dry cutouts on a cookie sheet in an oven set at less than 200 degrees until leathery, not brittle. Drill nutmegs on a cutting-board surface as directed on page 32. If using fresh bay leaves, strip the leaves from the branches and discard the stems.

Thread needle with the fishing line or thread and make a loop at the other end. Push the needle through the center of a bay leaf and slide it to the end of the string. Follow with bay leaves for 2 inches, then add a nutmeg, a cinnamon heart, a cinnamon star, another heart, and another nutmeg. Return to bay leaves and repeat this pattern, or one of your own choosing, making sure to finish with bay leaves.

To end, remove the needle, tie a loop, and knot securely.

Remembering

When Linda Kaat had her farm in Chester County, Pennsylvania, it was the kind of bed-and-breakfast gem that travelers have hoped to find since the bed-and-breakfast idea came to this side of the Atlantic. At Christmas, the long curvy road to the farm was lit by 26-point Moravian stars on wide front porches and candles in the windows of houses along the way. The farmhouse was a historic stone dwelling built as the country seat of a Philadelphia merchant.

When you arrived, fireplaces were glowing in the guest rooms. Fresh flowers welcomed you and the English oak furniture wore a high polish. The big room on the third floor was a favorite, a quiet retreat facing the back of the property. There, at the top of the house, you woke up in the morning to the sound of sheep bells from the flock grazing in the pasture beyond the green lawns and ancient holly trees. Downstairs in the long center hallway, the Christmas tree was so tall it dusted the ceiling. Its ornaments were fam-

ilies of lambs and sheep. Around the base of the tree, sweet fresh hay took the place of a tree skirt. At night, in the light of the chandelier, the tree was reflected in the glass panes of the front and back doors as you paused at the bend of the stairway to catch one last look before bedtime. Then, in the morning, there would be friendly chatter around the French toast and sausages, followed by goodbyes and promises to return and keep in touch. Linda would fill your car with fresh-cut holly piled over the tops of the suitcases, just clearing the back windows, and you'd be on your way, back down the curvy road and going home again.

Romantic Rose Strings

FRENCH ROSE BUDS

Cheering up the month of June with their beauty and fragrance, lavender and roses remain favorites among old-fashioned flowers. Nowadays, we seldom think of either one as culinary plants, as they once were, or as being particularly useful beyond making potpourri and flower arrangements. Yet medieval monks, like the mystery-story character Brother Cadfael, made tinctures and conserves and long-simmering syrups of rose petals that were used to treat ailments from migraine to melancholy.

From Queen Victoria's day until only a generation or two ago, white-gloved ladies frequently gathered for afternoon tea. At a cozy tea party, rose-petal jam or lavender-flower honey might have been offered with warmed scones and hot buttered toast. For more elegant teas, frosted cakes were decorated with crystallized rose petals, which you can make yourself by brushing fresh petals with beaten egg white, then dipping them gently in sugar. In those days, very grand dinners went on for six courses or so, with the salad served after the entree and a savory served after the sweet. The sweet, simply dessert to us, might well have been ice cream made at home of thick cream delicately flavored with rose petals or lavender flowers.

At school, young ladies were taught to use flowers to make pretty things—handiwork, as they would have said. These school girls made lavender "bottles" by

bending back the stems when the flowers were
blooming to perfection to form a "cage"
around the blossoms, which are then
woven through with silken ribbons.
Recipes for lavender bottles, some-

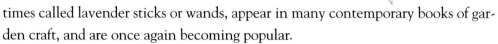

times called lavender sticks or wands, appear in many contemporary books of garden craft, and are once again becoming popular.

Another of the old schoolgirl handicrafts, not so well known, is making rose
beads. Roses were crushed into a mash, then blended with ground spices and a fixative to be rolled into beads and strung. The results of rose-bead making are less
predictable: The beads often turn out to be a dreary brown and none too fragrant.
Perhaps the greater difficulty in getting good results is why rose beads have not yet
had their revival.

Making rosebud strings is one of the remnants of Victorian civility we can
enjoy today, however, thanks to the availability of commercially dried rosebuds.

Mothers and daughters, with their own poetic imagination, can make this ut-
terly feminine string together. Rosebud strings make memorable party favors for
birthday celebrations and bridal showers. For a pretty variation, you can alternate
rosebuds with soft-colored beads, available at most craft stores.

Like making rosebeads, drying rosebuds at home is impractical, even if your
garden is bursting with roses. The rate of spoilage far exceeds the rate of success,
and the small pink rosebuds, called boutons, sold by herb suppliers are just too perfect not to use.

> Over the winter glaciers
> I see the summer glow,
> And through the wild-piled snow drift
> The warm rosebuds below.

> —*Ralph Waldo Emerson*

to make one 24-inch Hearthstring

Thin needle with a large eye
32 inches nylon fishing line or strong sewing thread
1 cup (about 2 ounces) whole dried rosebuds
36 faux pearls, each 8–10 mm in diameter

To assemble

Thread the needle and tie a loop at the opposite end. Push the needle through the center of a
rosebud and slide it to the end of the string. Add a
faux pearl and slide to the rosebud. Repeat to the end.

To end, remove the needle, tie another loop,
and knot securely.

ROSES AND LEMON LEAVES

A big unruly shrub of Harrison's Yellow roses grows near the two windows on the south side of our kitchen. One day before the June roses were in full
bloom, the bush was visited by a black-and-white-capped bird otherwise so entirely, so brightly yellow you had to smile to think he had selected a yellow rose on
which to perch! In my twenty-odd years of bird watching in this spot, I've seen
countless cheerful phoebes, goldfinches, and ruby-throated hummingbirds, but
this new visitor prompted a trip to the worn old Audubon guide. The visitor was a
yellowthroat.

ROMANTIC ROSE STRINGS

Along with attracting birds, there are so many reasons to grow roses, a flower universally loved, the inspiration of writers and poets. But they make serious demands on the gardener, with their need for pruning and spraying. And even the most successful growers have only modest luck at drying whole rose heads because their density frequently causes them to rot from within before the outer petals are crisp.

To make this Hearthstring, you need to seek out professionally dried roses if you want a long-lasting garland, though for a brief use at a party or wedding celebration you can use fresh roses. There is no rule that you need make a long-lasting Hearthstring each time, so perhaps a fresh string is something to make on impulse when your roses are at their peak. String them and enjoy them for a day or two just as you would a corsage or a fresh floral bouquet, and when they look spent, toss them out and that's that!

On the other hand, if you do decide to make a long-lasting string from professionally dried roses, you will find exquisite dried rose heads on the market. Strung up with glossy salal, as lemon leaves are also called, they will produce an elegant string. In keeping with the elegance and festive spirit of this string, finish each end with sumptuous bows of wired French ribbon with long graceful streamers.

YOU NEED

to make one 30-inch Hearthstring

1 bunch (about 300) lemon leaves
Long sewing needle with a sharp point
38 inches strong sewing thread or nylon fishing line
12 perfect dried roses, cut from their stems
1 yard wired French ribbon

ROMANTIC ROSE STRINGS

Strip the lemon leaves from their branches and discard stems.

Thread your needle and tie a loop at the other end. Fold a lemon leaf horizontally, veins and stem inward, into 3 or 4 pleats and push the needle through the center of the pleated leaf. Push leaf to the end of the string and repeat until you have a section of leaves 2 inches long. Push the needle through the center of a rose and slide it next to the leaves. Repeat with alternating sections of leaves and a rose until everything is strung, making sure to end with leaves.

To end, remove needle, form another loop, and knot into place. Cut ribbon in half, fashion each half into bows, and tie to the string at either end next to the leaves, leaving the loops free for hanging.

Remembering

We love to fill our homes with collections that are bits of our lives—family pictures and familiar little mementoes from the places where we grew up. In my kitchen window sit a little painted horse brought from Sweden and a clear glass bottle filled with rose geranium syrup made lovingly by my friend Mary Milligan. All these things, with special memories attached, make our homes the scrapbooks of our lives.

Mary's herb room is full of treats made with her herbs. For the kitchen, she flavors brandy with tarragon and vinegar with horseradish. Her mustard pickles and candied angelica stems are famous among her friends. One of Mary's best herbal specialties is her rose geranium syrup. She warns that it really does take four days and the gift of patience to make it properly. It is, as the old saying goes, a labor of love.

After roses, violets, and lavender, perhaps the most beloved of old-fashioned flowers is the rose geranium (Pelargonium graveolens). Scented geraniums are a large group of tender perennials whose leaves have an amazingly intense perfume. Scented geraniums can smell of limes, strawberries, and all manner of good things, but the true rose geranium is one of the oldest and the most lovely.

"If you were born with a romantic nature,
all roses must be crammed with romance."
—Vita Sackville-West

MARY'S ROSE GERANIUM SYRUP
(Serve over the very best vanilla ice cream)

Place 60 to 70 washed rose geranium leaves in 3 cups of boiling water. Remove from heat and let stand until a "tea" is brewed, then transfer to the top of a double boiler and simmer the tea over hot water, gradually adding a cup or more of sugar. Simmer for several hours. Stir occasionally. Remove from heat.

Allow the mixture to steep overnight. Repeat the simmering, gradually adding a few tablespoons of additional sugar, then repeat the steeping overnight three more times. To retain the deep red color and rich taste of the rose geranium, take no shortcuts! This process truly does take four days to get the best results and it is well worth it.

When thick and syrupy, pour into washed, sterilized bottles and seal. Give lovingly, as Mary does, to your friends.

Woodland Strings

HEMLOCK CONES

The best part of making a string of hemlock cones is going for a woodland walk to forage for the cones. If you come upon them unexpectedly, fill your pockets, or plan your expedition and bring a gathering basket to fill. Everyone has a favorite basket, and mine is a traditional Sussex garden trug. These trugs are handmade in a small village south of London, across the Downs in the direction of the Channel coast. Only a few families still practice this old basketmaking craft. They begin by cutting willow branches for the body of the basket and chestnut, from the stands along the hedgerows, for the rims. The wood is planed, wrapped around a mold, and steamed, then nailed in shape to form a basket. Queen Victoria popularized the trug, and it is still the most popular sort of gardening basket.

With your trug or your own favorite basket, set out on a woodland path and look for some velvety bits of fresh moss to gather, along with some fallen cones in addition to the ones you gather for the string. You can use them to make a simple understated woodland wreath by gluing them onto a grapevine base. If you happen upon some acorns, hickory nuts, or other interesting cones, put those in the basket for your wreath too. American larch (*Larix laricina*), also called tamarack, produces cones in a ruddy mahogany shade that grow up to three-quarters of an inch long. Larch cones also make a handsome string, on only a slightly larger scale than the hemlocks.

YOU NEED
to make one 3-yard Hearthstring

4 cups (about 75) hemlock cones
Thin needle with a sharp point
116 inches strong sewing thread

TO ASSEMBLE

Thread your needle and tie a loop at the opposite end. Stab the needle through a cone at an angle, as shown in the drawing, and slide it to the end of the string. Repeat until all cones are strung.
To end, remove the needle, tie another loop, and knot securely.

Wildings
(Ebenecook, Maine, 1969)

Blueberry, bunchberry, nestled in moss,
Juniper bristle and wintergreen gloss,
Seedling first-needling and just an inch high,
Under me, tapestry, over me sky—
Under me, tapestry, over me sky,
Crying his being, a sea gull goes by—
Drawn to his passing, I kneel in the dew.
Bunchberry, red berry, blueberry, blue . . .

—*Elisabeth W. Morss*

BLACK-EYED SUSANS

Some wild flowers are too fragile, or too nearly extinct, to be dug up in their natural growing place and brought home to the garden. But the ox-eye daisies and black-eyed Susans that thrive along the roadsides and in every meadow—they are fair game! However, transplanting them can be frustrating. These wildings thrive in the most inhospitable, neglected places, behind abandoned buildings or in vacant lots—even in the cracks of city sidewalks. Still, once they are disturbed, they often obstinately fail to take hold. But, like feverfew (*Chrysanthemum parthenium*), another plant with a daisy-like flower, or the yellow daisy called dyer's camomile (*Anthemis tinctoria*), once they do accept their new surroundings, watch out! These sun-loving plants, so innocent to look at, bake in the summer sun like a lazy snake, then seed themselves with abandon. They must be thinned ruthlessly.

Everyone loves daisies. You can plan a succession of daisies for your garden. Begin with the short-stemmed English daisies (*Bellis perenne*) in springtime and continue all summer long.

By June, common field daisies are so prolific that school girls used to weave them into long chains to carry at graduation ceremonies. In August, black-eyed Susans abound. In minutes, you can walk out into a meadow and gather an armful to take home. Put some in an ironstone pitcher for the kitchen table. Learn to make them into chains as a late-summer variation on the old daisy-chain theme. Sit out in a sunny spot with a great jug of lemonade and your wide-brimmed hat to string black-eyed Susans and capture the sheer bliss of summer afternoons with nothing whatsoever to do but soak up the sunshine and celebrate your vacation days.

About 50 black-eyed Susans
Thin needle with a large eye
44 inches strong sewing thread or nylon fishing line

To assemble

Cut the stems off the black-eyed Susans close to the head of the blossoms. Use the flowers as soon after picking as possible, as the petals become fragile and the heads brittle in only a short while.

Thread your needle and tie a loop at the other end. Pierce a flower with the needle from the head down through the stem and slide it to the end of the string. Repeat until all flowers are strung, leaving as little room as possible between blossoms.

To end, remove needle, tie another loop, and knot into place. The flowers will look fresh for a day, or you can allow them to dry. The color remains vivid.

Remembering

Van Mund lives in Connecticut, on an unpaved road that leaves the highway, then turns across a grassy plain with a small river winding through it. Down the road you cross a set of tracks, the kind that look like a train comes by once a month. Next you go past a big colonial farmstead not far from the birthplace of Nathan Hale. After rounding another bend, you see a path leading to a gray shingled house surrounded by herbs and flowers. If you go around to the back porch, there are sure to be kittens. Nearly always, one is nestled on an Adirondack settee by the door. If you knock, Van might answer. But probably not!

Most often, she is out in the woods or searching the meadow to see what's in bloom. Van gathers grasses in June; later in August, she fashions tansy leaves and grapevines into pineapple-shaped wreaths that she designed one summer with her daughter Leslie.

By September, she's up the road just a little farther to see her neighbor Ginette. Together they ramble down through Ginette's woods to the trout pond. There they watch the friendly, greedy fish jump up for the food Ginette tosses out into the water. On the way back, Van and Ginette usually fill their arms with feathery green ambrosia. Ambrosia, Van's favorite, is the tricky herb that pops up in the spring in no relation to where it was planted. Ambrosia seedlings look like miniature trees, with little leaves that are soon lost in the fast-growing seed heads. Van dries ambrosia and the wild American pennyroyal, herbs that smell as fragrant dried as they do in the garden.

In October, Van meets another friend and they drive off for an annual ritual, sharing a day picking long tendrils of bittersweet. Van picks carefully—just the most perfectly shaped strands will do. Her friend is faster and less selective. Close by there is the sound of water and the setting is quite perfect. When they begin to tire and the car is nearly full, Van usually says, "Another time we must go and pick bayberries or chive blossoms." Van celebrates all the seasons harvesting things that grow on Brigham Hill.

She shares some flowers with Margery for her inner-city church fair and some with Mary Ellen just for friendship's sake. Some gatherings go in her butt'ry. No matter where her wild pickings go, Van has an special glow when she's out in her gardens or her woods. Gathering nature's gifts is her secret weapon against all life's cares.

Scrapbook Strings

ADIRONDACK MEMORIES

Adirondack-style twig furniture is made from tree limbs with bark and gnarls intact. Its comfortable style is popular far from the unspoiled wilderness area in northeastern New York State for which it is named. The Adirondack region is a vast place of wild beauty, with chains of clear, cold lakes, around which the air smells of pine forest. You can drive for miles and miles without passing another car or entering a town. It is an area out of another time, undeveloped, a rich jewel preserved amid a crowded corridor of urban sprawl.

In the Adirondacks, the word "camp" refers to any of the region's country retreats built by industrial barons near the turn of the century. These wealthy magnates furnished their "camps" with simple furniture in the Arts and Crafts style. In the unspoiled woods, they canoed on the lakes and found patches of wild pearly everlasting along the edges of the pine forests. They and their families spent the summer capturing the romantic ideal of going back to nature.

With more realism than romance, the American painter Winslow Homer painted Adirondack deer hunters and starkly beautiful fishing scenes from his family's camp in the mountains. The Adirondacks are full of harsh contrasts and nostalgic summer memories.

Your own patch of woods—even your neighborhood park—can provide bits of mossy bark, lichen-covered twigs, cones, and white birchbark fragments (good for color contrast) for your own version of this woodland string. Of course, never strip bark from a living tree! Save a tree whenever you can, and never harm one if you can help it. Forage for a basketful of materials Mother Nature has already left for you on the forest floor. Stop to look up at the trees when you take to the woods. See the incredible wonder of the sky, and listen to the bird song. Don't forget to keep your eyes open for the unexpected. Found objects will make your woodland string uniquely your own.

GATHER AND HARVEST

Acorns with tight-fitting caps
Soft brown hazelnuts
Shiny buckeyes
Chestnuts and hickory nuts
Curling white birchbark
Soft sheets of moss
Lichens and seed pods

YOU NEED
to make one 28-inch Hearthstring

½ pound (about 300) fresh or dried bay leaves

Thin needle with a large eye

36 inches strong thin twine with a rough, earthy texture

A basketful of woodland foragings, including hemlock cones, birchbark, and moss-covered twigs

TO ASSEMBLE

If you are using fresh bay leaves, strip the leaves from the branches and discard the stems.

If you are using buckeyes or acorns, they will need to be drilled (see page 32).

Moss-covered twigs should be fresh and pliable, otherwise they may require drilling as well.

Thread your needle with the twine and tie a loop at the other end. Push the needle through the center of a bay leaf and slide it to the other end of the string. Repeat with a few more bay leaves, then establish your own pattern of foragings alternating with bay leaves, making sure to end with bay leaves. To end, remove needle, tie another loop, and knot securely.

CAPE COD MEMORIES

"If you love the sand dunes and salty air . . ."

Singing about old Cape Cod, people will all at once break out into wide smiles. Sometimes, their eyes will mist over just thinking about beach plums and clam shacks, once visited or often dreamed of. It happens from Boston to the Pacific! Your own favorite stretch of seashore, perhaps far from Cape Cod, can yield all you will ever need to create a beach-memories string, even if Waquoit and Wellfleet are just words to you.

In Maine, at the mouth of the Kennebec River, with the constant beam of the Sequin Island lighthouse offshore, a long sandy beach on an otherwise nearly rocky coastline yields tiny crab legs washed ashore with the tides. The tides also sweep in blue-black skate-egg sacs and chunks of wood looking like soft rocks, with their surfaces worn smooth by the river in its rush to meet the sea. What flotsam of beach life do you remember from your special place, having walked, pail in hand, to gather seaside treasures along the water's edge with the sandpipers for company? We nearly all have been shell seekers at one time or another—at Cape Cod, at Sanibel, or near Point Reyes.

Having fun making a memory string with children beats a trip to the souvenir shop every time! There are many unspoken lessons to learn as you gather and string up found objects. Nature's gifts are the best gifts, and lessons like these, learned from happy experience, are remembered long after all the no, no, no's of parental wisdom are forgotten.

BEACHCOMBINGS

Soft gray driftwood chunks
Blue mussel shells
Colorful dried sea weeds
Black skate-egg sacs
Stark white shells
Fragrant bayberry leaves
Evergreen cones washed ashore
by the sea

Seashells are fun to gather for Hearthstrings because you must be a careful beachcomber, a real sleuth, to find some that the sea has already cut holes in through which you can run your needle and twine. As you wander and gather with children, teach them how fragile the shoreline is. Caution them never to pick living plants, disturb terns or other nesting birds, or climb the dunes that can slide away so easily, breaking down the ecological balance. Take great deep breaths of salt air while you look for ospreys overhead. Don't forget to protect yourself from the sun's rays with a wide-brimmed hat!

For a true Cape Cod string, use the fragrant leaves of bayberry (*Myrica pensylvanica*), "one of the truly North American plants the settlers found," according to garden historian Ann Leighton. Its berries have a waxy gray coating that is used to make fragrant soft green bayberry candles. Often, it was called candleberry. Not a seasoning and not to be confused with culinary bay leaf, the Cape Cod bayberry should be used strictly for decoration and fragrance. Because it grows wild in the sandy soil of the Cape, it is a nice alternative to bay leaf for a Cape Cod Memories string, but if it is not available to you, turn to culinary bay for your own version of this project. If you use driftwood, soaking it and using it wet helps when piercing it with the needle. Playing a cassette tape of sounds of the sea may be inspirational!

to make one 36-inch Hearthstring

½ pound (about 300) fresh wild bayberry leaves or fresh or dried bay leaves

Tapestry needle with a large eye and a blunt end

44 inches strong coarse twine

1 beach pail full of beachcombings, including hemlock cones, seashells, and driftwood

To assemble

If using fresh bay or bayberry leaves, strip leaves from branches and discard stems. Thread the needle with the twine and tie a loop at the other end. Push the needle through the center of a leaf and slide it to the end of the string. Repeat with more leaves until you have a section 3–4 inches long.

Follow with a shell or a piece of driftwood and continue until you have a section of beachcombings 3–4 inches long. Establish a pattern of alternating leaves and beachcombings and follow it to the end, making sure you end with the leaves.

To end, remove the needle, tie another loop, and knot securely.

There is a perpetual mystery and excitement in living on the seashore, which is in part a return to childhood and in part because for all of us the sea's edge remains the edge of the unknown; the child sees the bright shells, the vivid weeds and red sea-anemones of the rock pools with wonder and with the child's eye for minutiae; the adult who retains wonder brings to his gaze some partial knowledge which can but increase it, and he brings, too, the eye of association and of symbolism, so that at the edge of the ocean he stands at the brink of his own unconscious. —*Gavin Maxwell,* Ring of Bright Water

Sources

Dried Artichokes and Pomegranates

Rogers Herbs and Flowers
P.O. Box 8544
Porterville, California 93257
(209) 568-2735
Mail order only

The Herb Farm
Barnard Road
Granville, Massachusetts 01034
(413) 357-8882
Mail order
Seasonal list at Christmas $1.00

Dried Orange Slices

Lin Kilby Collection
9 Maple Avenue
Roseville Park
Newark, Delaware 19711
(302) 737-0339
Mail order list $1.00

Fresh Bay Leaves

Pecan Hill Farms
Route 1, Box 1244
Montgomery, Texas 77356

(409) 597-4181
Mail order list $3.00

Bay Laurel Farm
West Garzas Road
Carmel Valley, California 93924
(408) 659-2913
Mail order

Bulk Herbs and Spices

Attar
Playground Road
New Ipswich, New Hampshire 03071
(800) 541-6900
Retail shop and wholesale-only mail order

Frontier Cooperative Herbs
Herb and Spice Collection
3021 78th Street
P.O. Box 118
Norway, Iowa 52318
(319) 227-7996
Mail order

Herb 'N' Renewal
Rural Route 1
Laura, Illinois 61451

(309) 639-4145
Mail order catalogue $5.00

The Herb Shop
East Main Street
Lititz, Pennsylvania 17543
(717) 626-9206
Retail shop and mail order

Mountain Rose Herbs
P.O. Box 2000
Redway, California 95560
(707) 923-3941
Mail order list $1.00

Freeze-Dried Fruits and Flowers

Flowers Forever
311 East 61st Street
New York, New York 10021
(212) 308-0088
Retail shop and mail order

Opus Topiarium
980 Pacific Gate Unit 16
Mississauga, Ontario, CANADA
(416) 564-1797
Mail order list $3.00

Preserve the Memories
P.O. Box 351
Marion, Connecticut 06444
(203) 620-0477
Mail order

Fresh and Dried Chilies

My Santa Fe Connection
P.O. Box 1863
Corales, New Mexico 87048
(505) 842-9564
Mail order

Whitewater Farms
Box 41
McNeal, Arizona 85617
(602) 642-3624
Mail order

Dried Harvest Corn and Popcorn

Shari and Dick Swank
Swank Farms
601 Churchill Road
Hollister, California 95023
(408) 470-4704
Mail order

Hand-Dyed Sisal, Raffia, and Grass Twine plus Hand-Gathered Natural Materials

Christa Hobson and Clyde Middleton
Basket Beginnings
P.O. Box 54
Newark, California 94560-0054
(510) 226-0941
Mail order

Hemlock and Larch Cones

Wendy Neumeyer
Maine Balsam Fir Products
West Paris, Maine 04289
(207) 674-2094
Retail, wholesale, and mail order

Verdigris Paint Kits

The Pottery Barn
100 North Point Street
San Francisco, California 94133
(800) 922-5507
Mail order

Dehydrators

Electric dehydrators manufactured by Waring Corporation and American Harvest are available at Sears, J.C. Penney, Macy's, and Montgomery Ward stores nationwide.

Small Handmade Cookie Cutters

Gooseberry Patch
4 N. Sandusky Street
P.O. Box 190
Delaware, Ohio 43015
1–800–854–6673
Mail order

Old, Rare, Out of Print Books

Cate Olsen and Nash Robbins
Much Ado Books
7 Pleasant Street
Marblehead, Massachusetts 01945
1–800–800–MUCH
Retail Shop, Mail order, Search service

Unusual, Heirloom Seeds

Marilyn Barlow
Select Seeds
180 Stickney Road
Union, Connecticut 06076–4617
(203) 684–9310
Mail order
Catalogue $2.00